I0481602

HEART MANDALA
COLORING BOOK

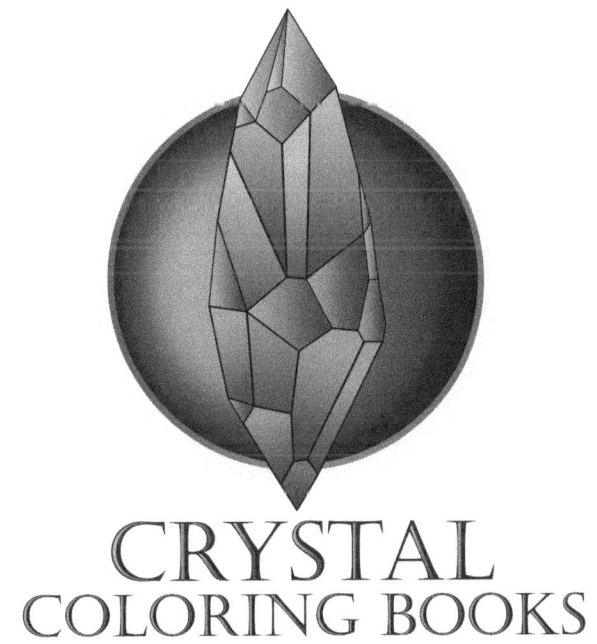

CRYSTAL
COLORING BOOKS

ISBN: 9781723783937

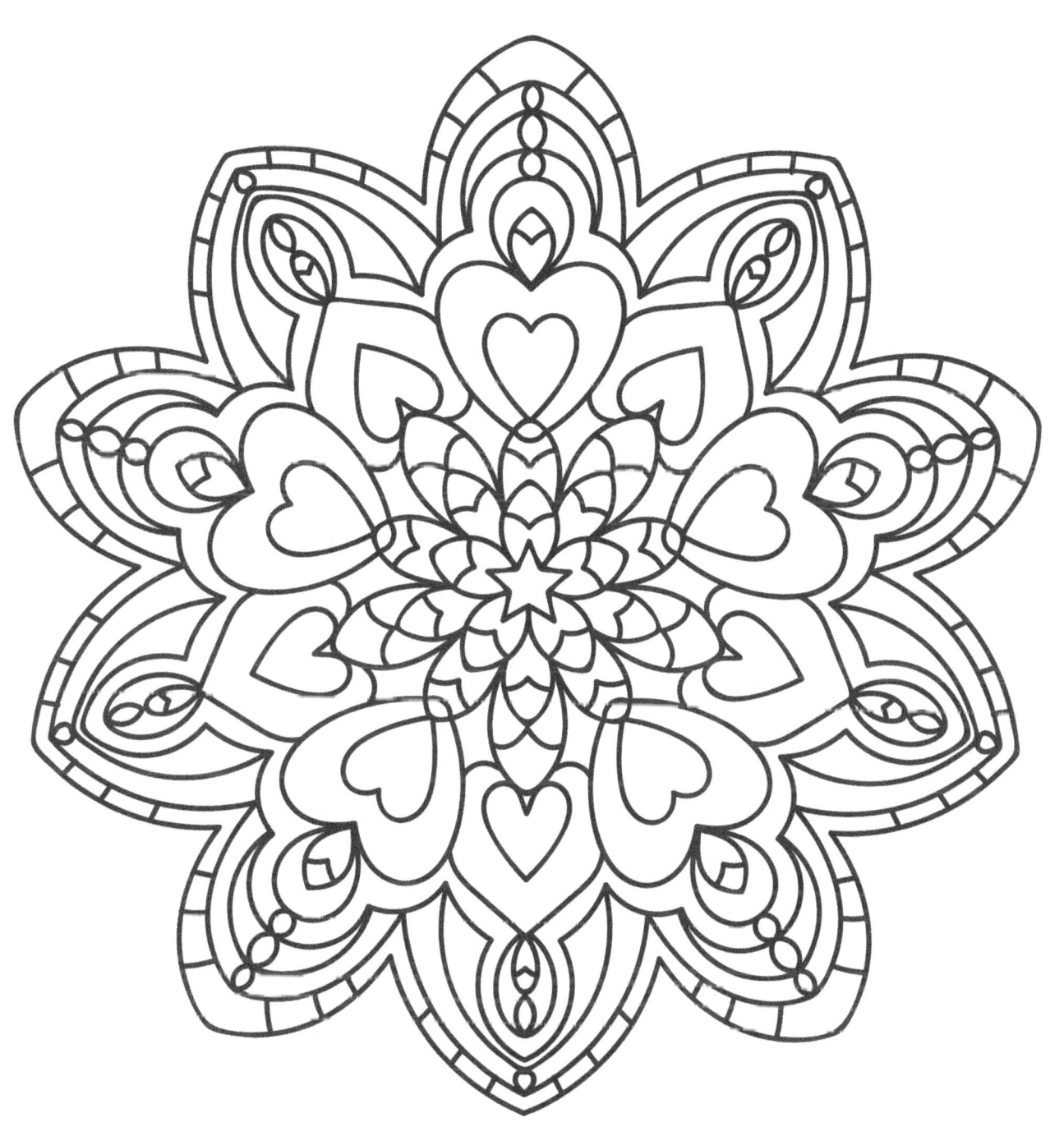

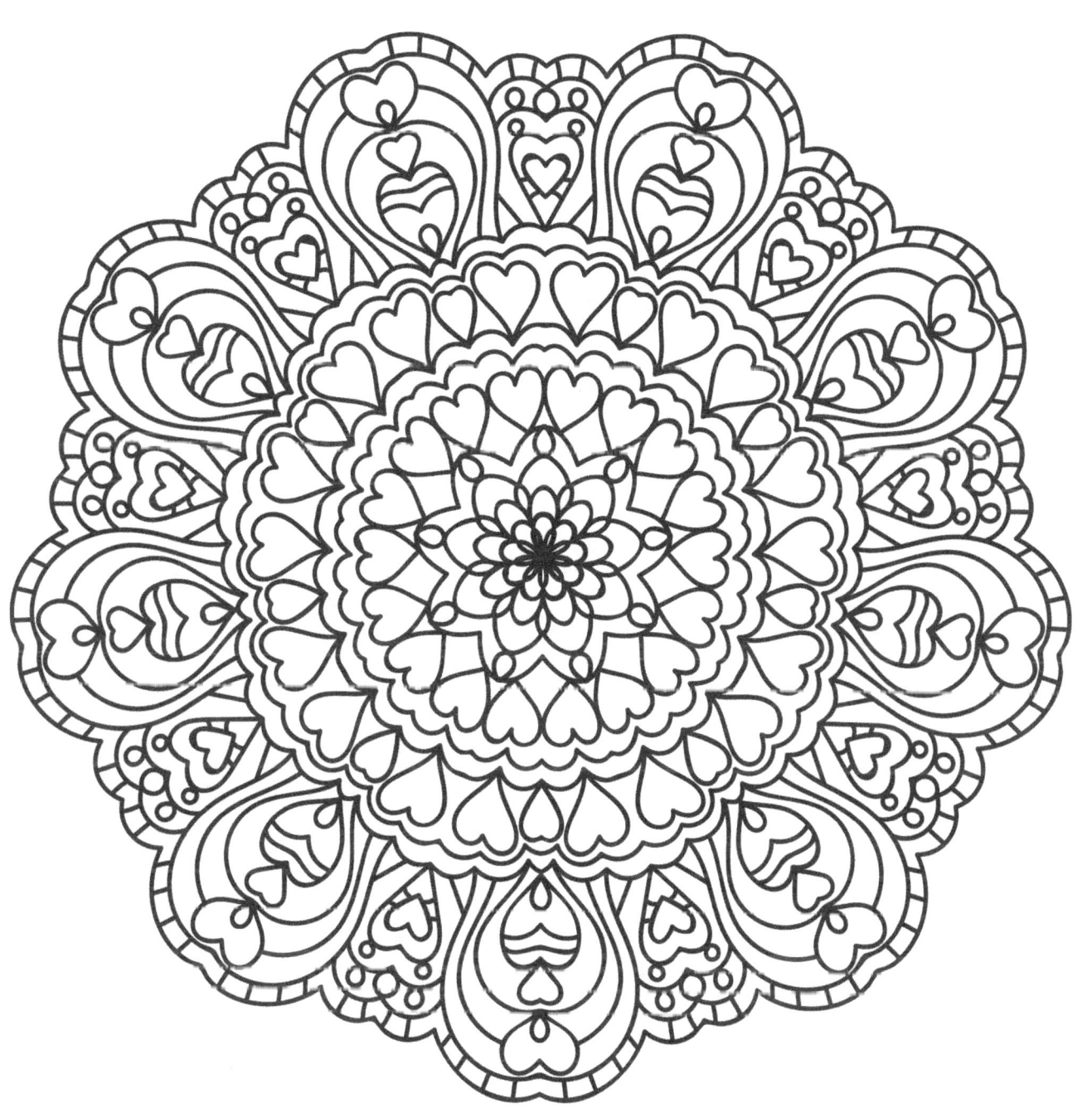

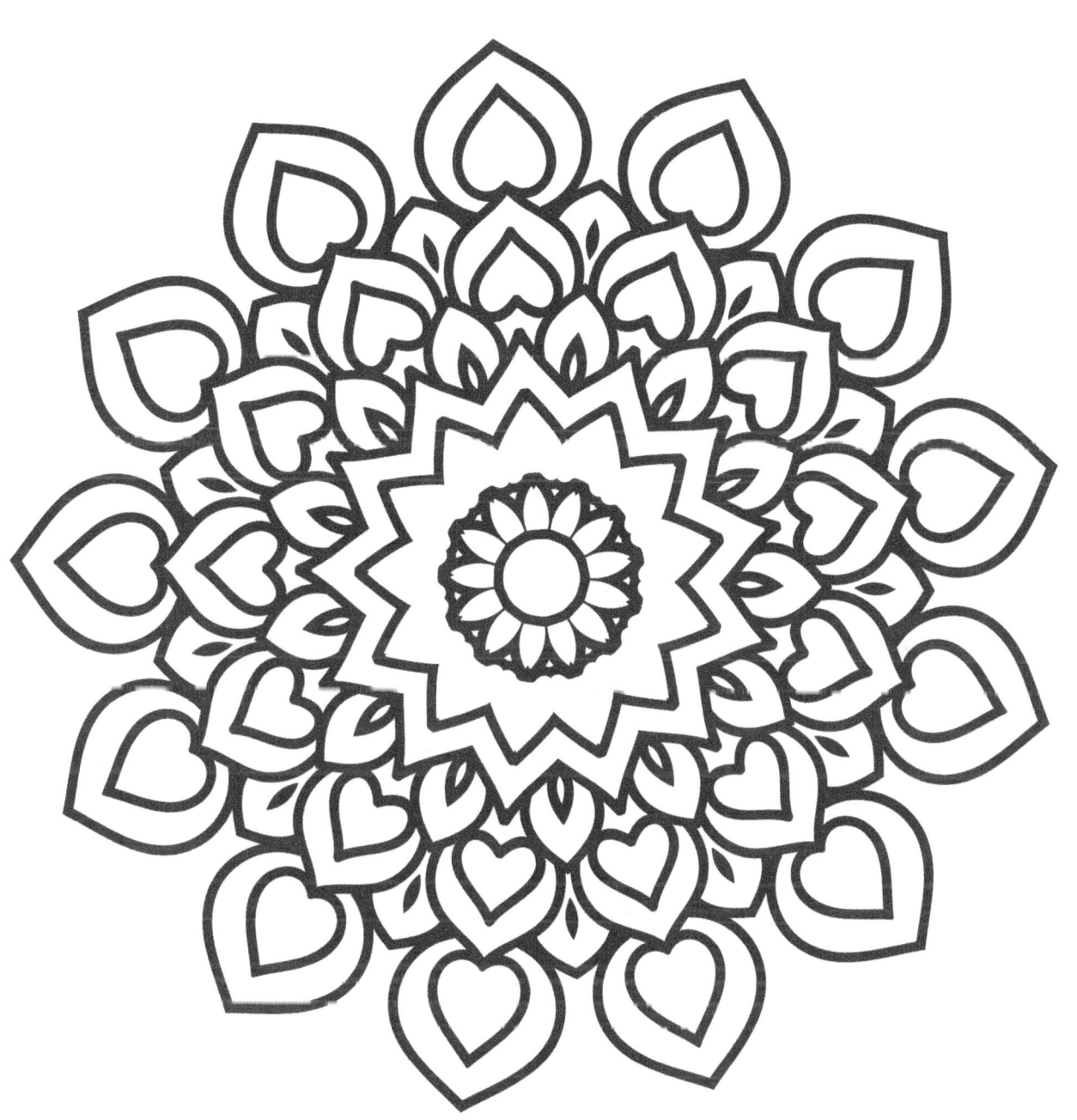

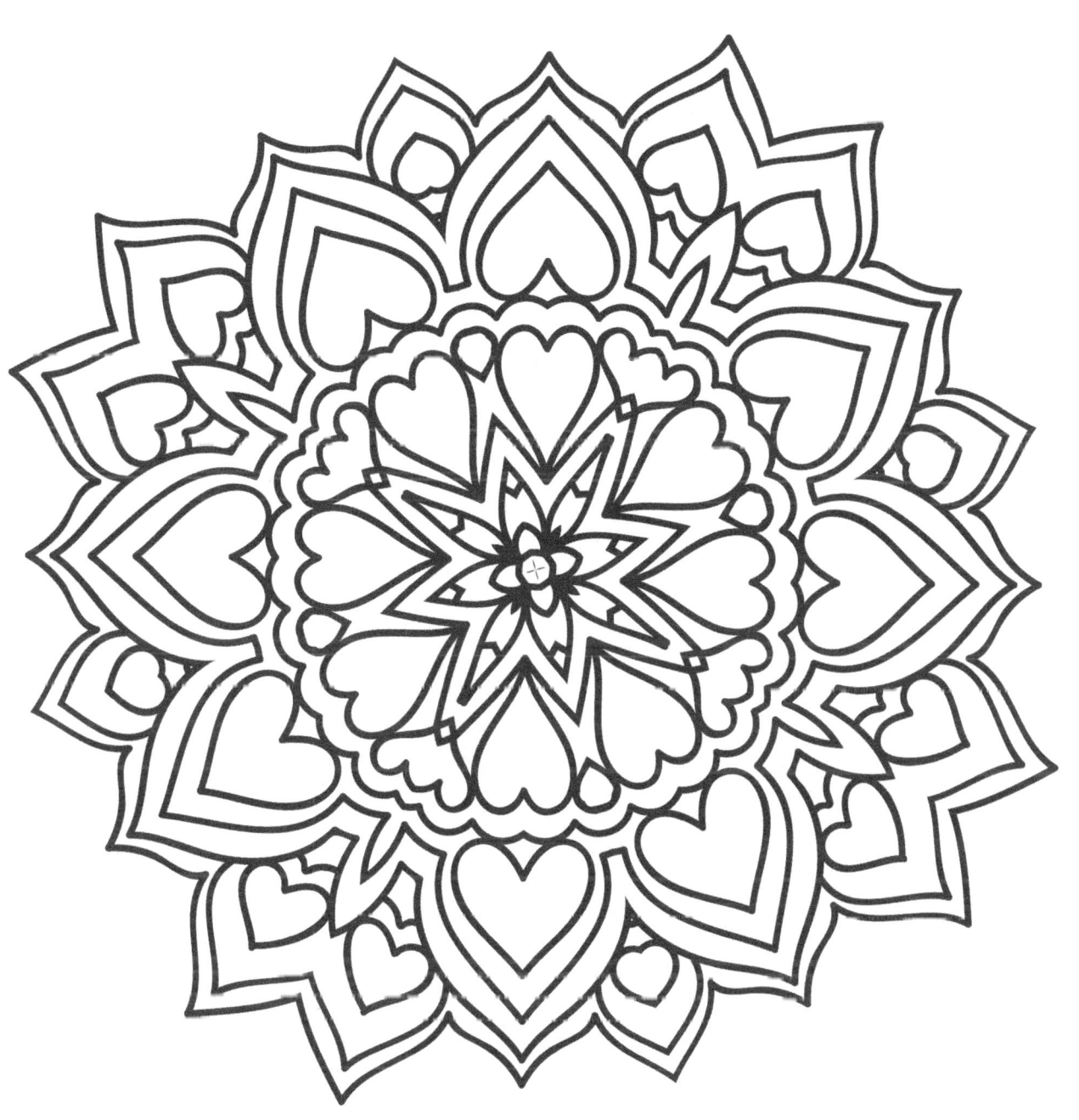

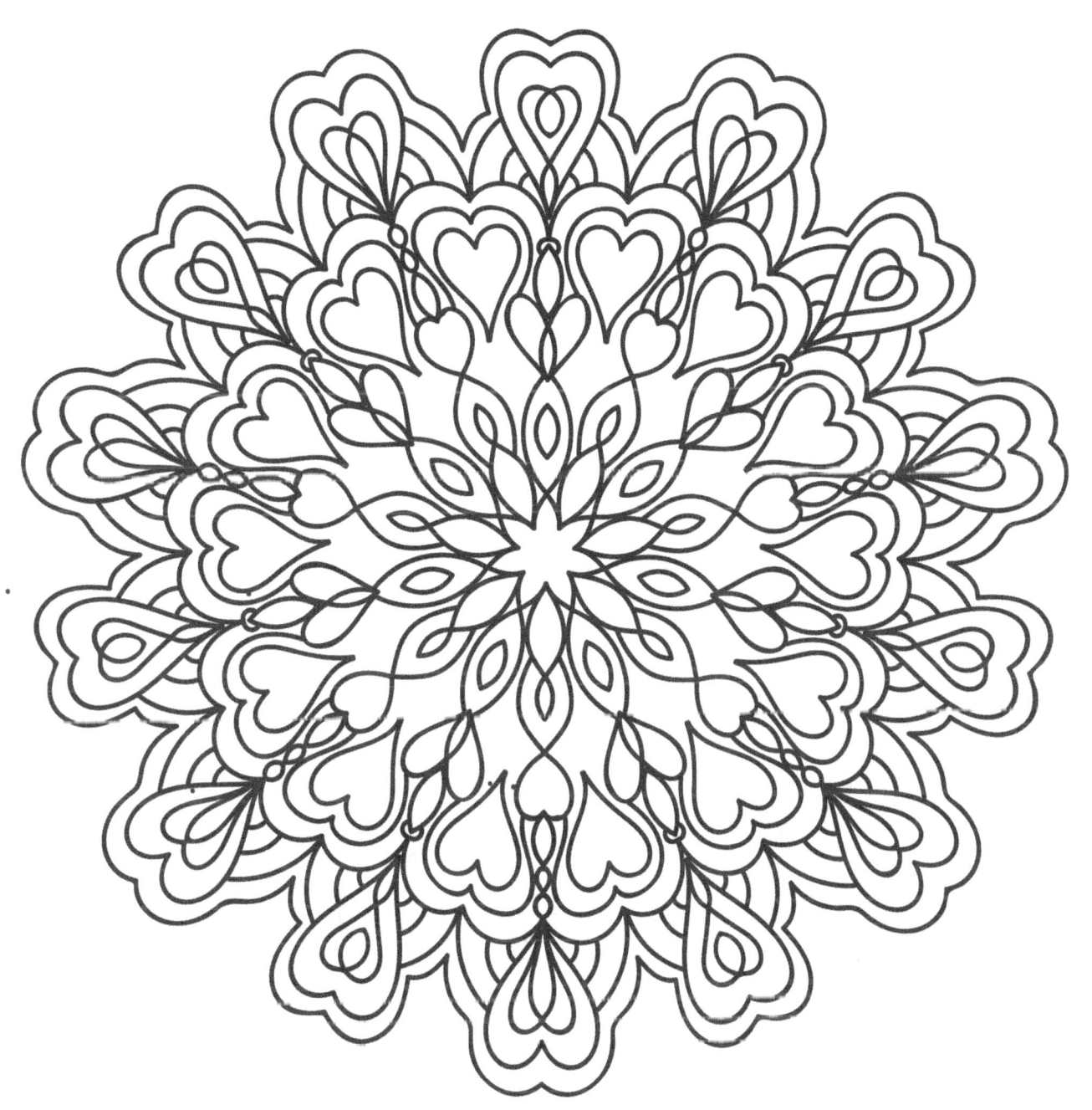

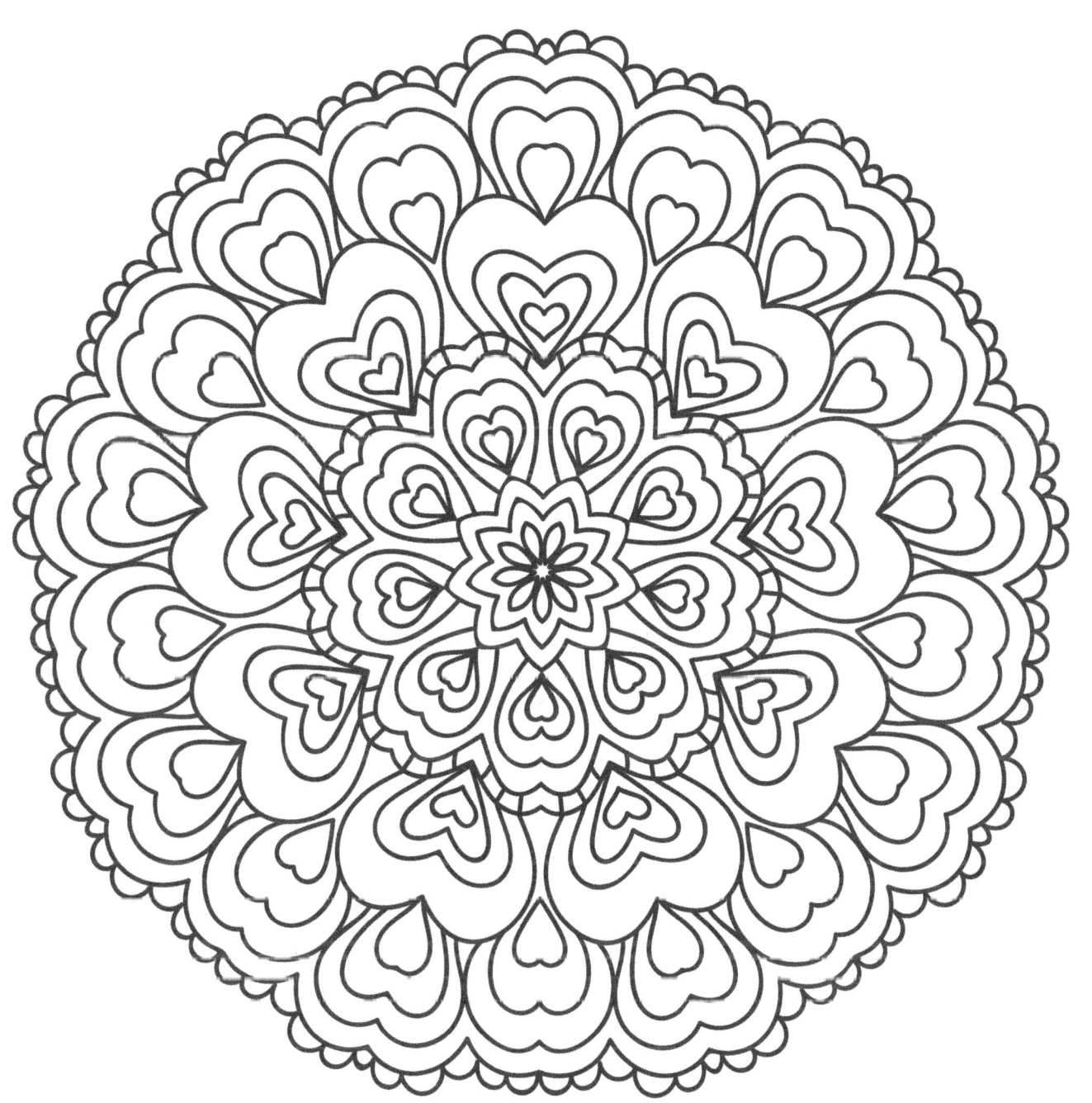

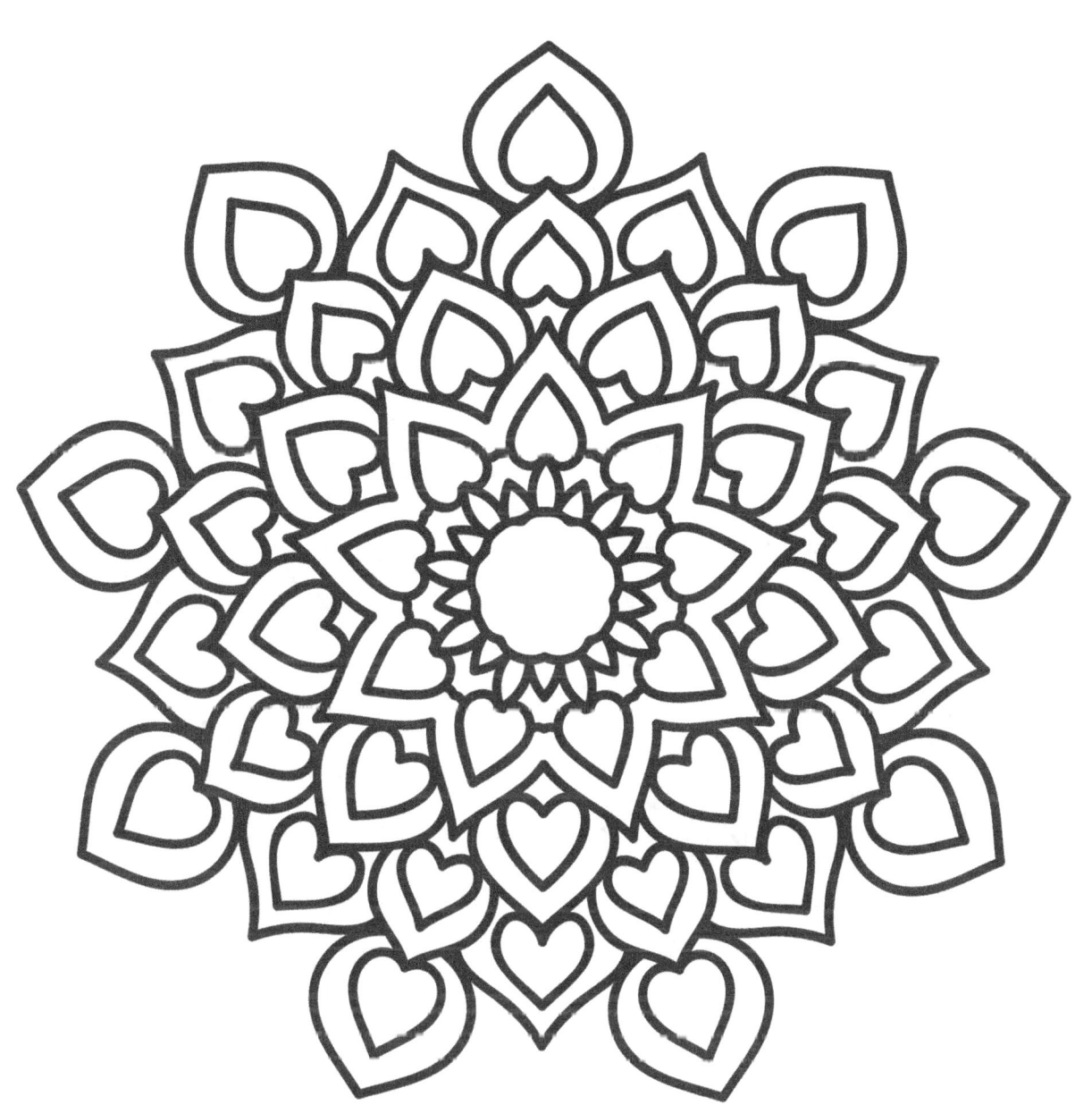

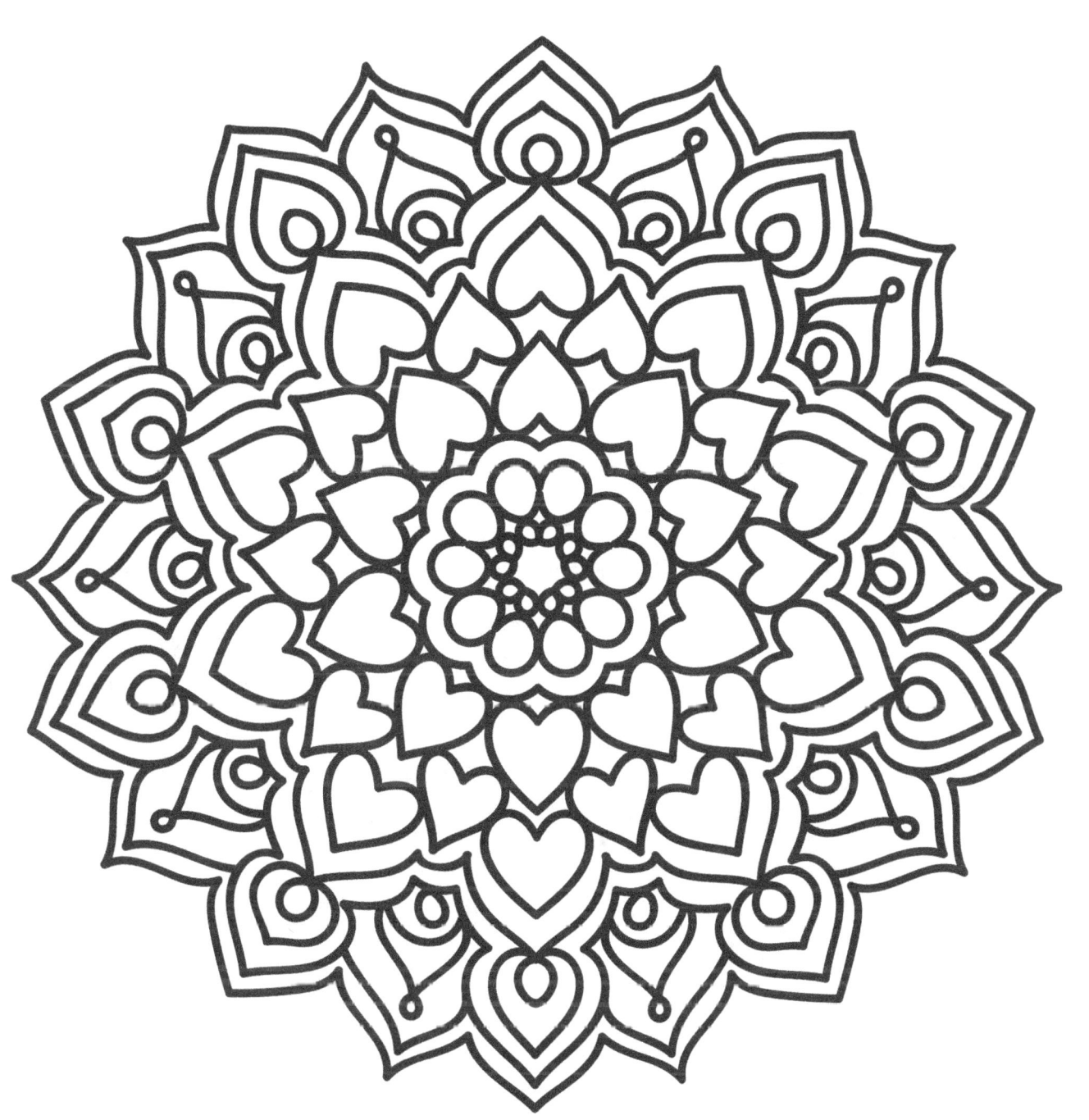

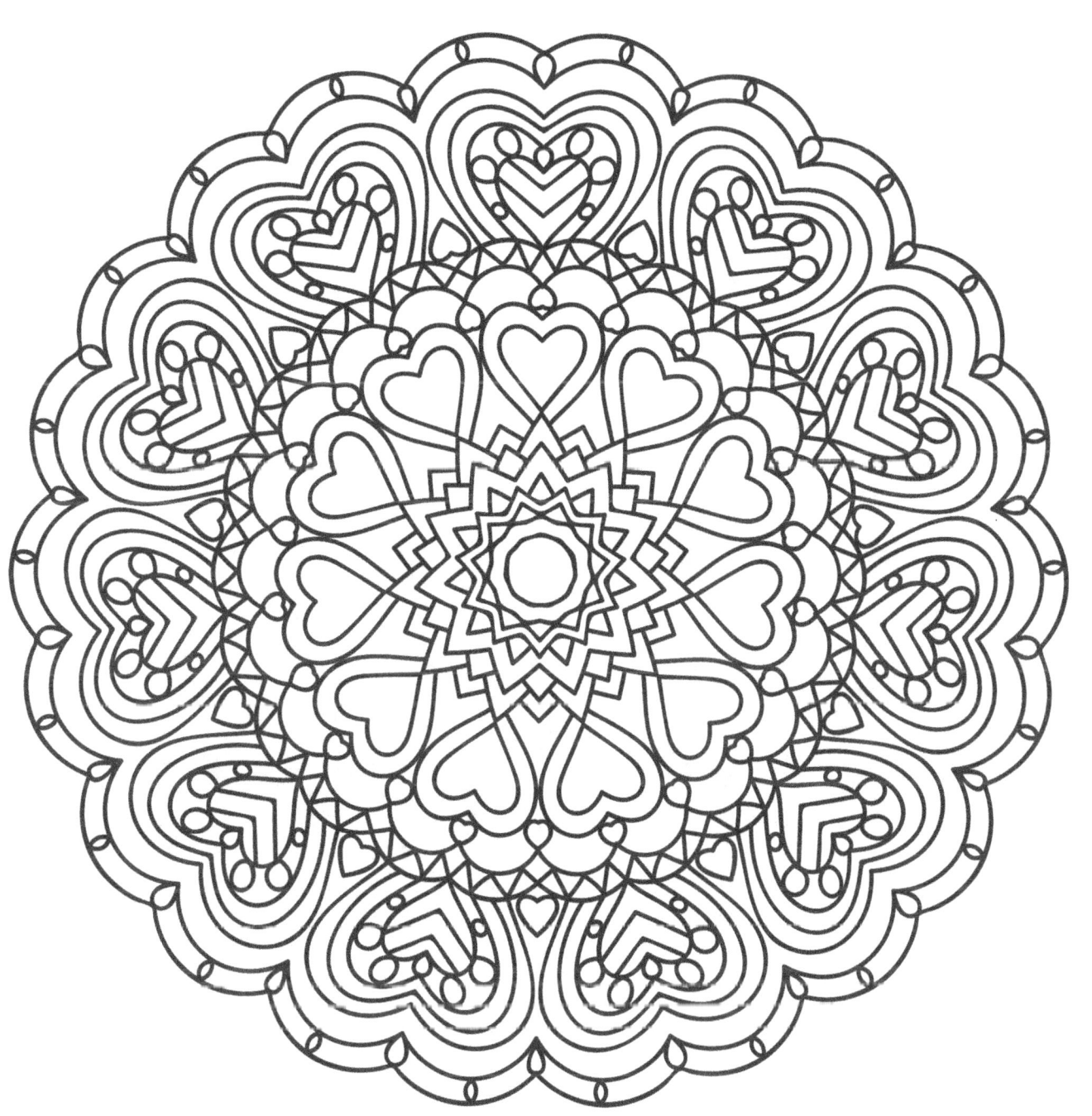

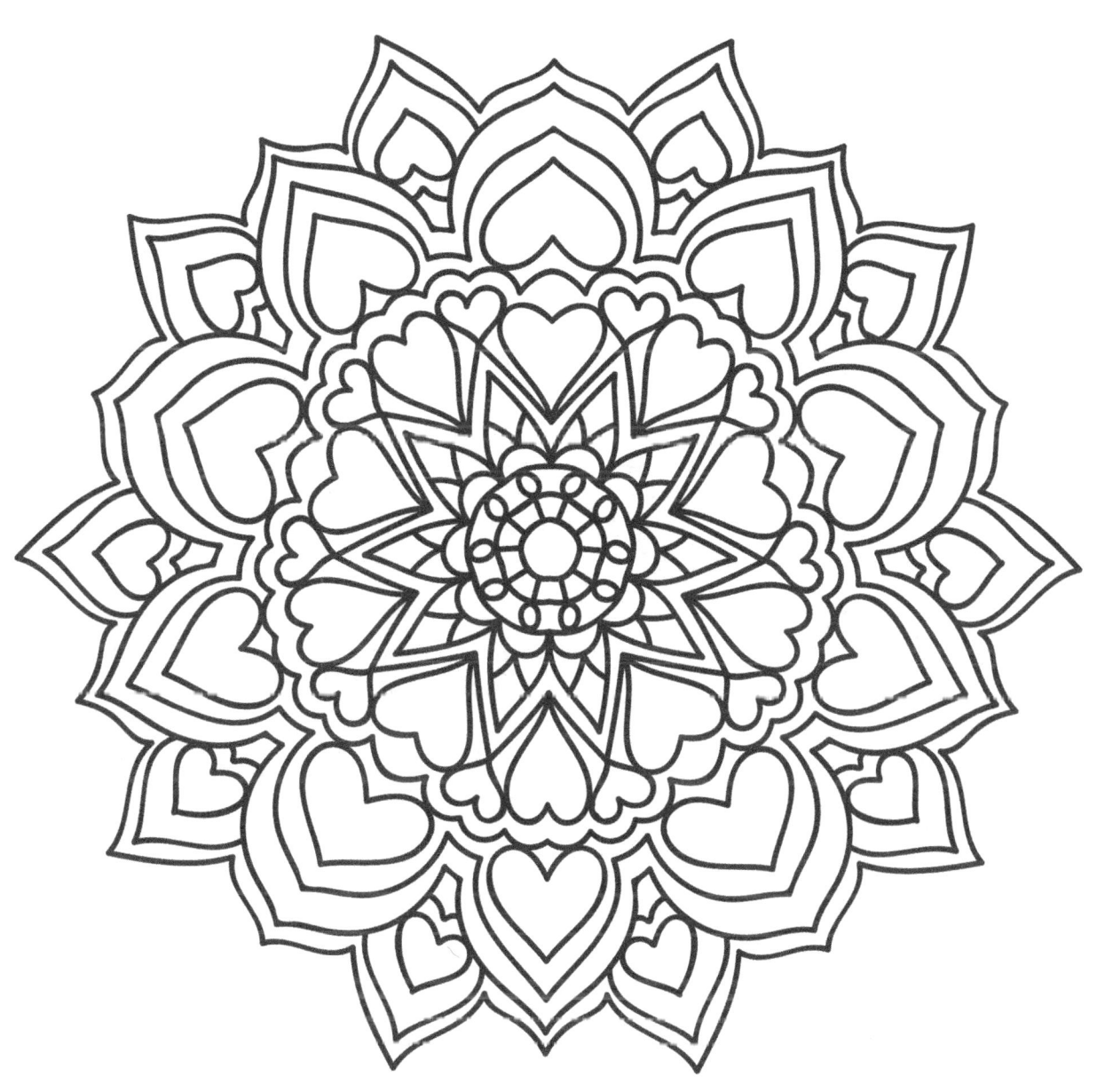

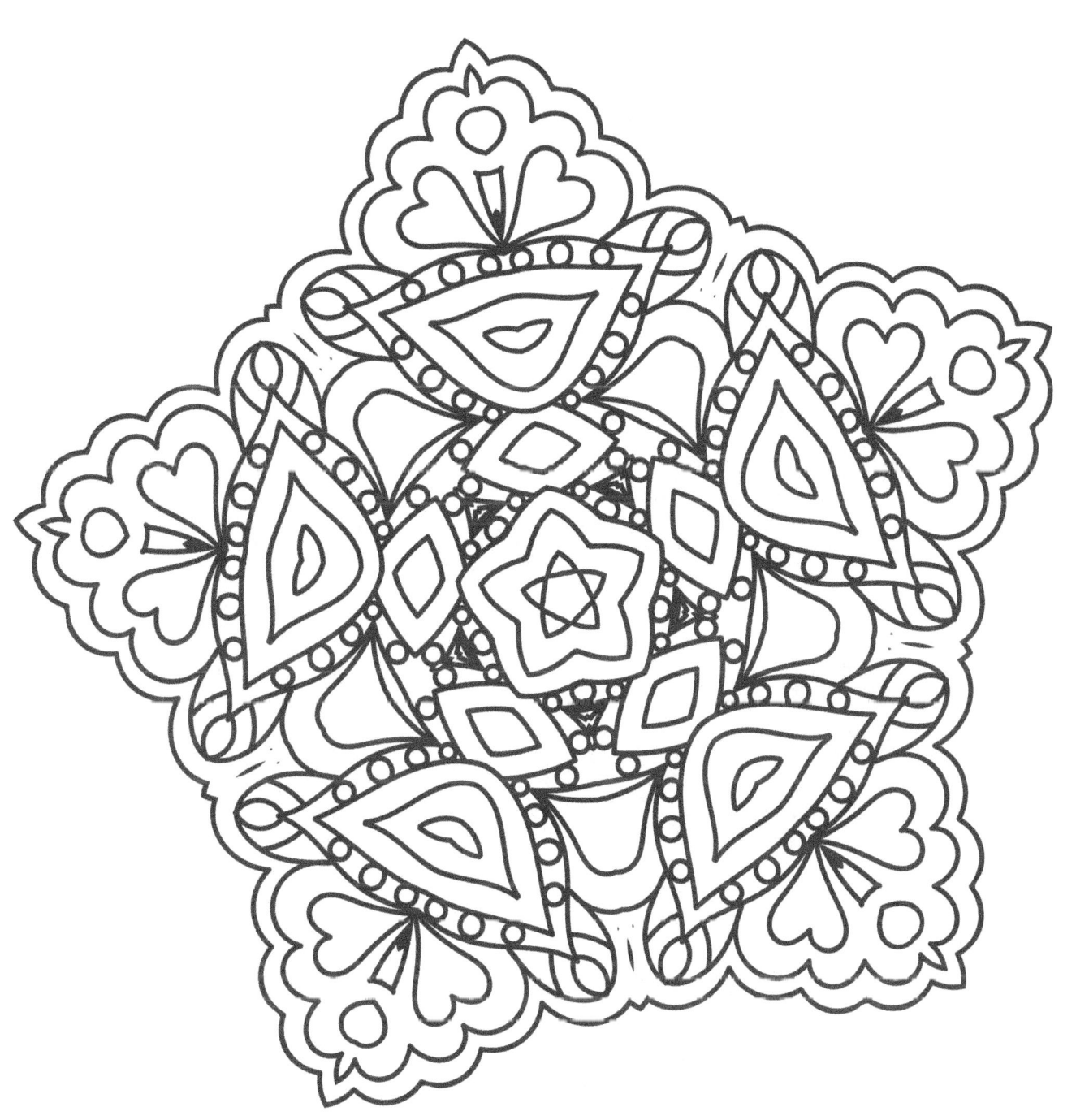

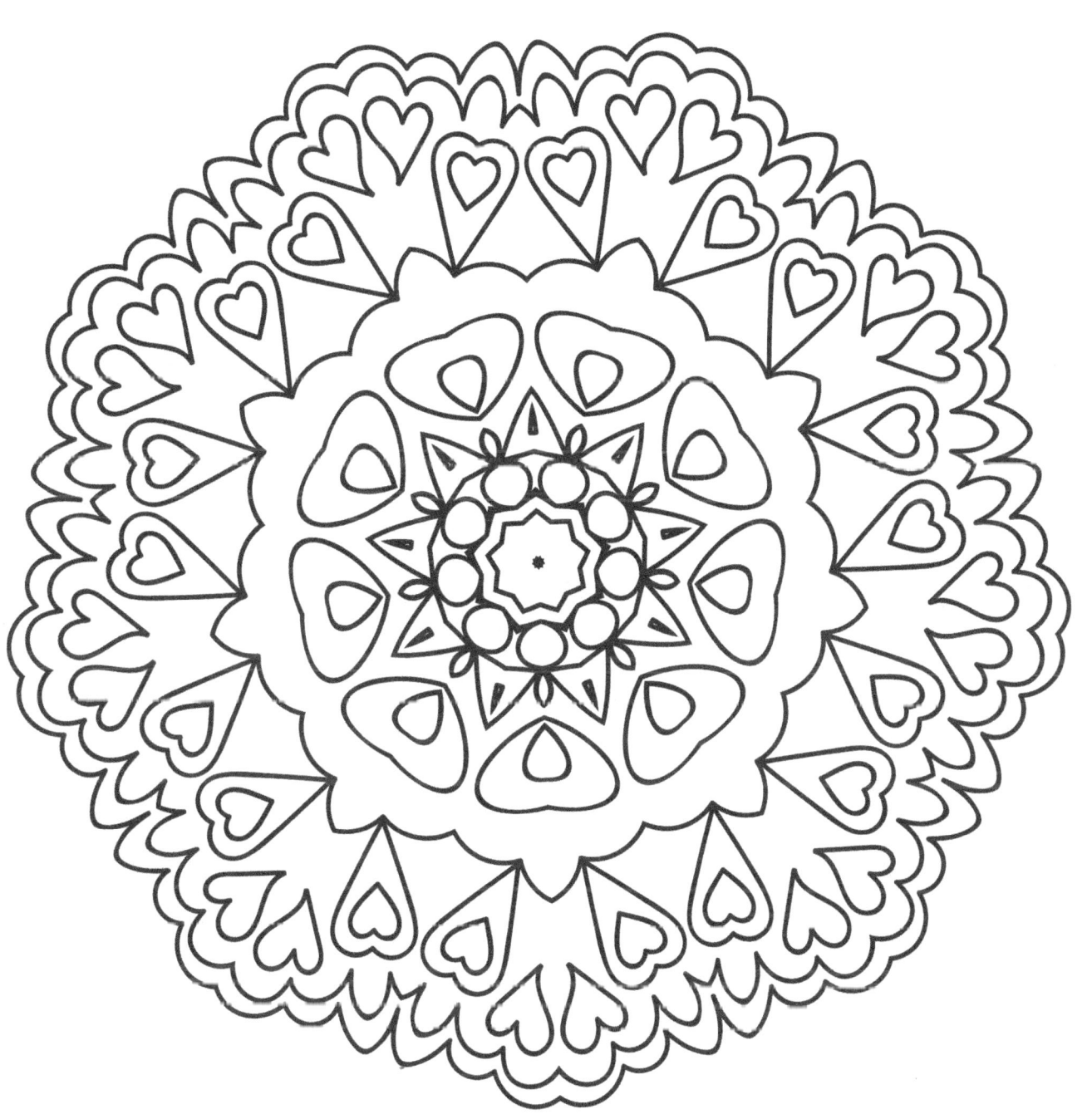

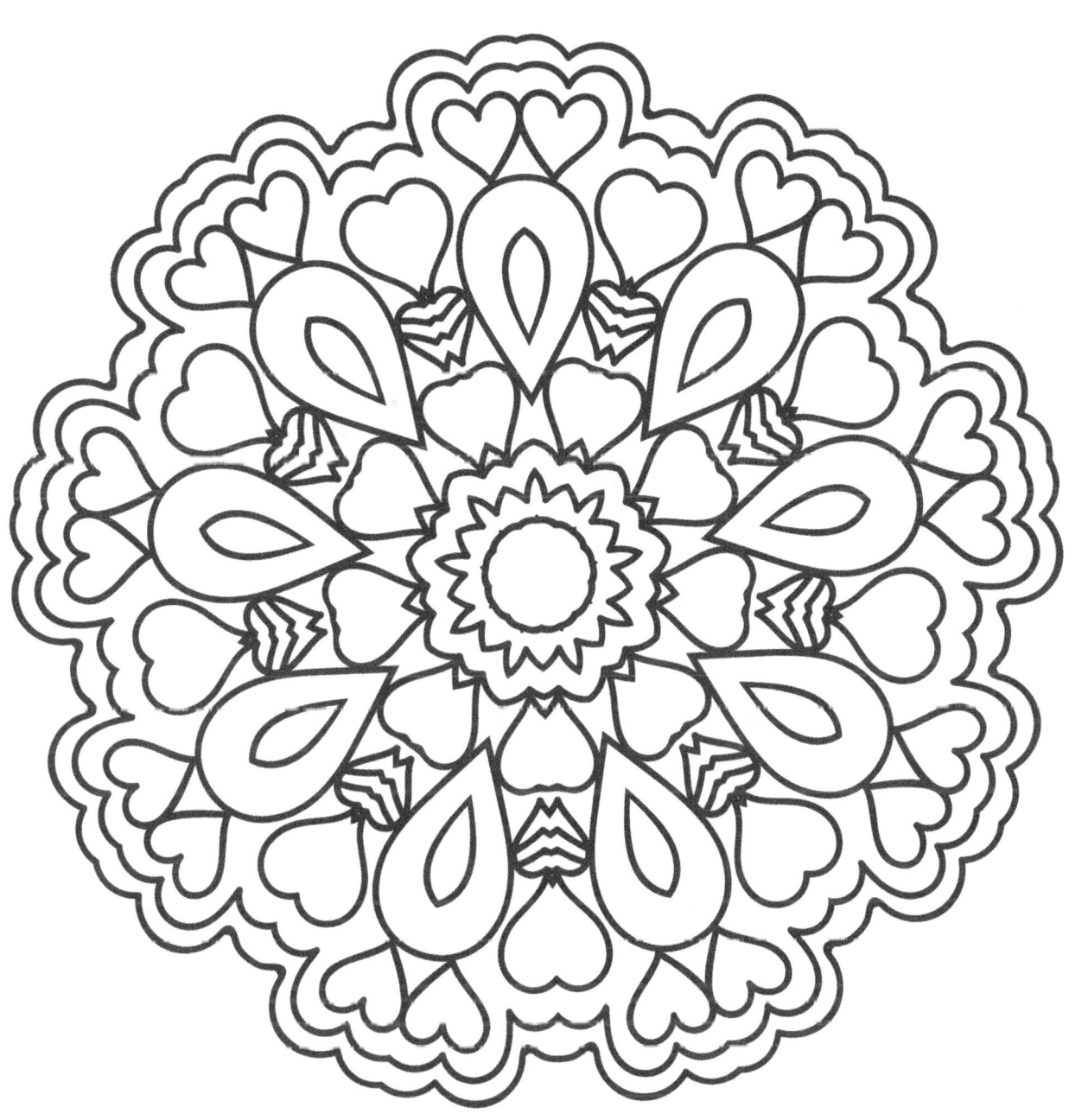

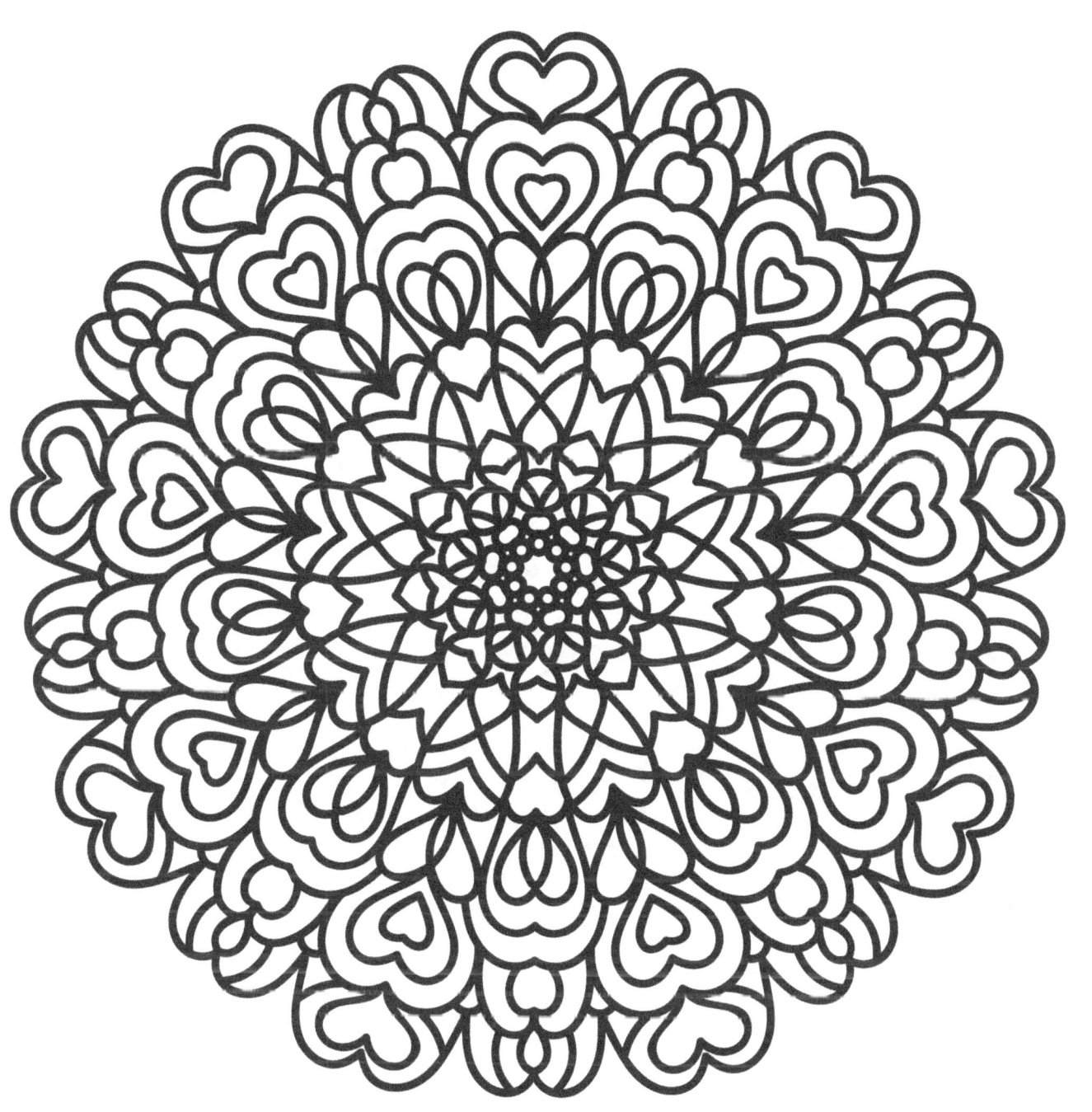

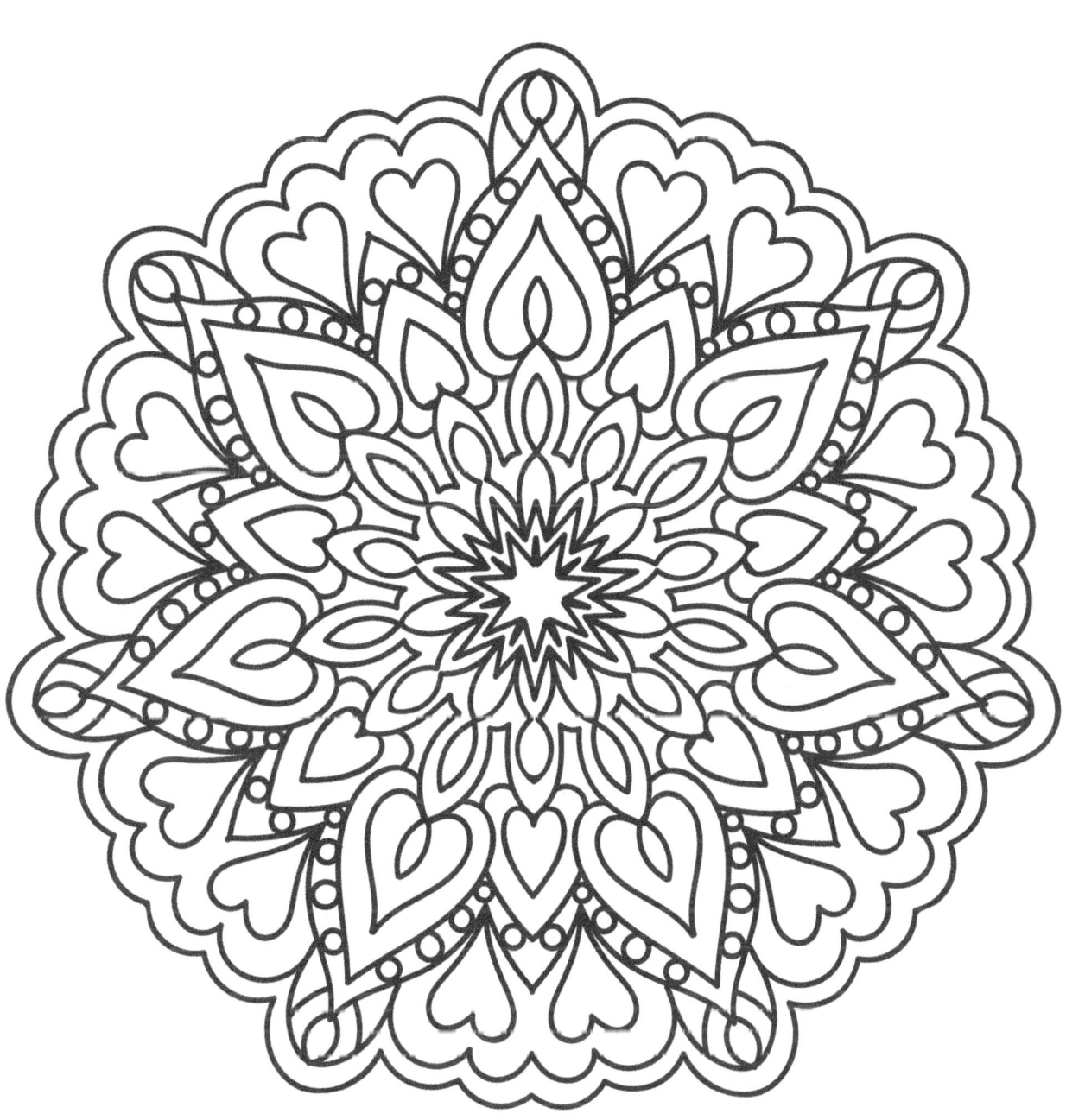

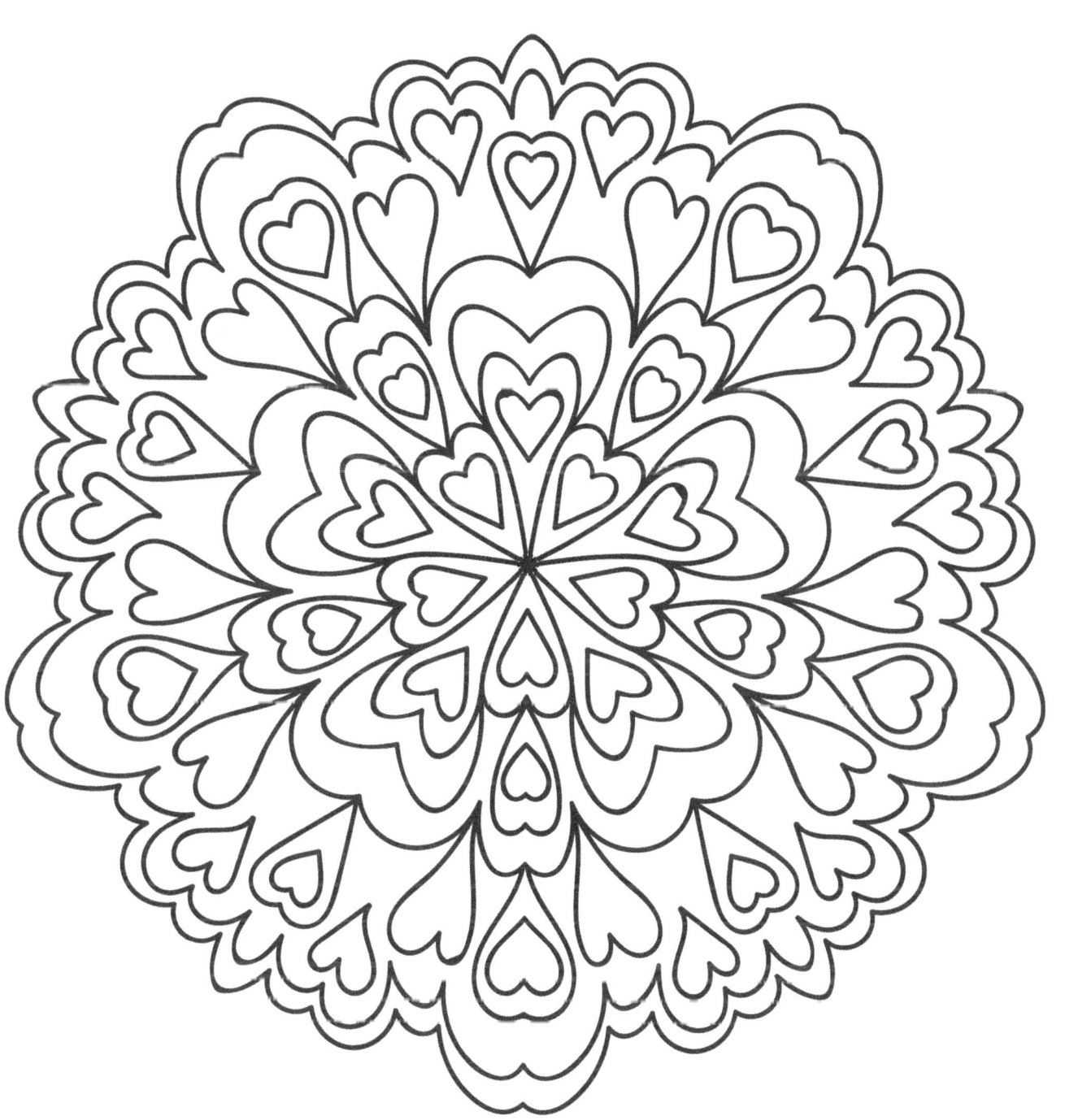

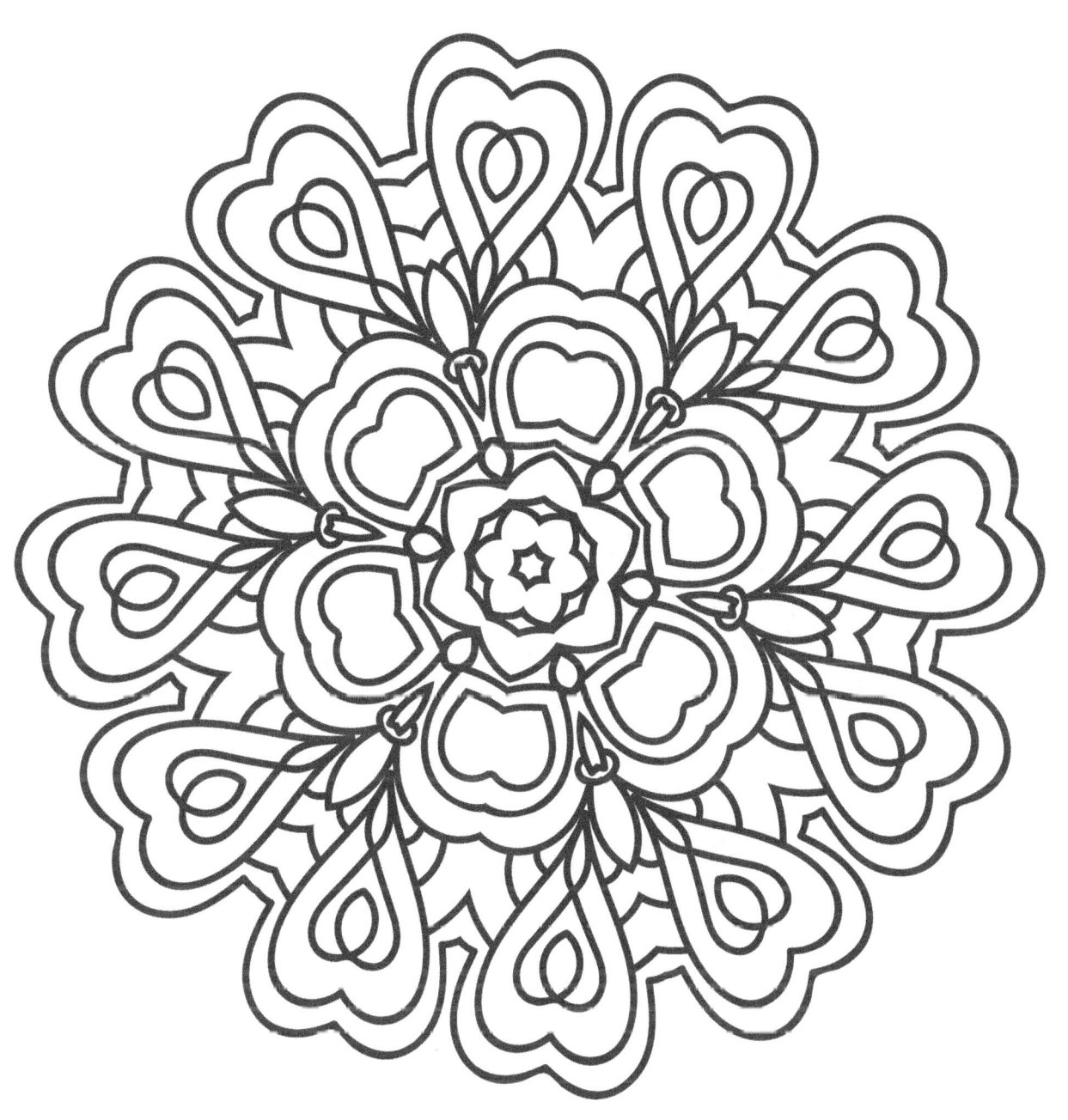

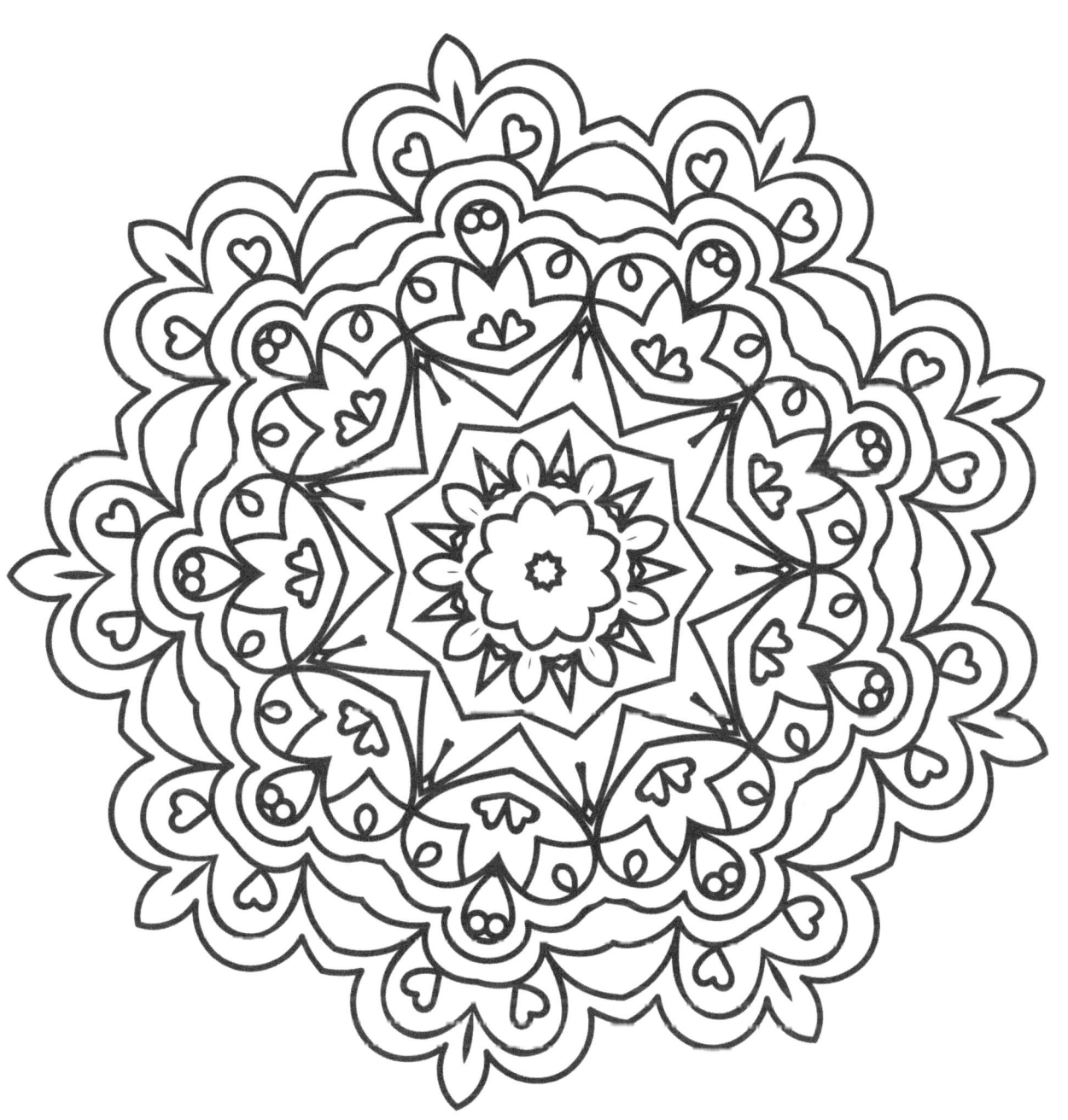

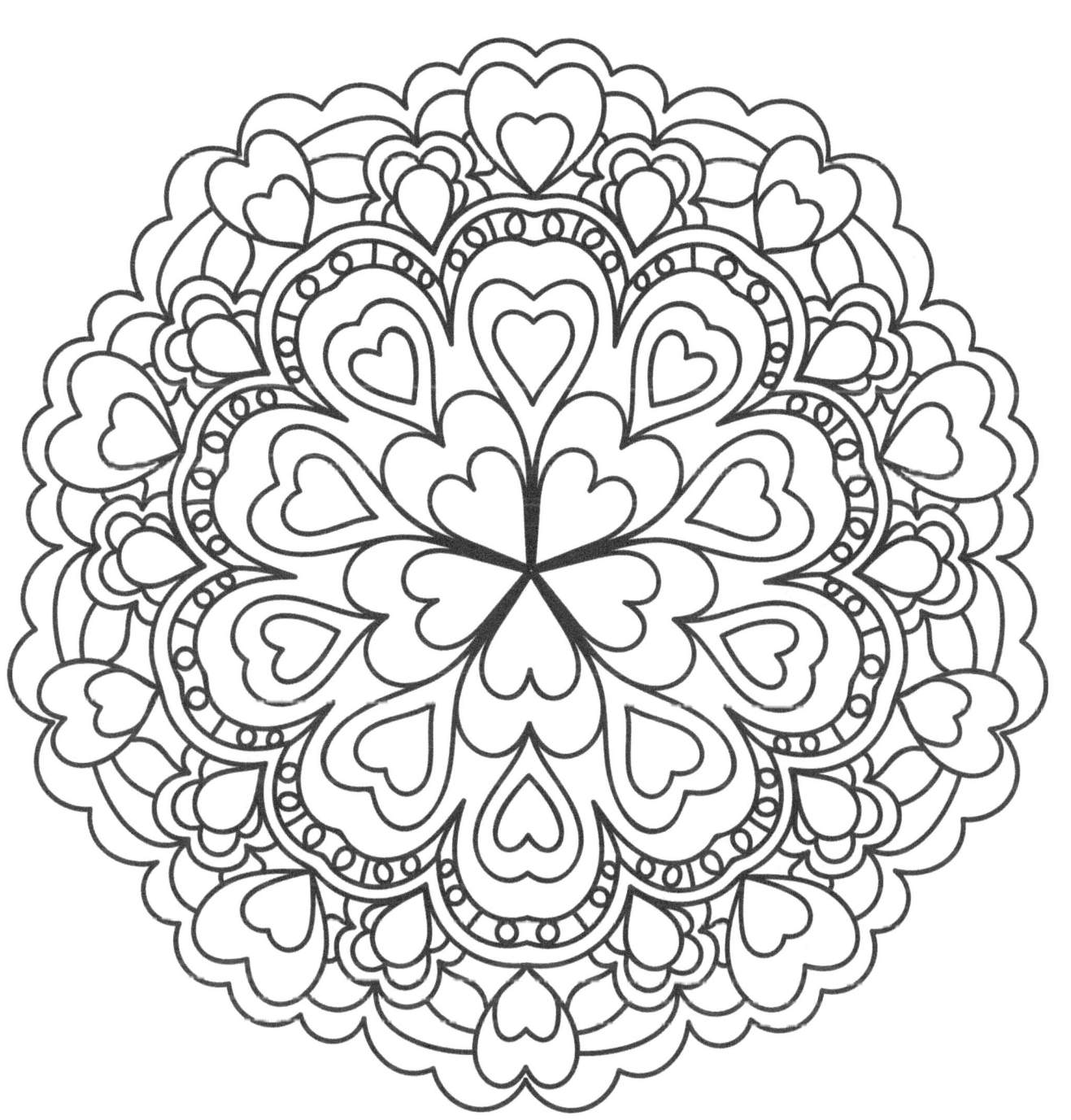

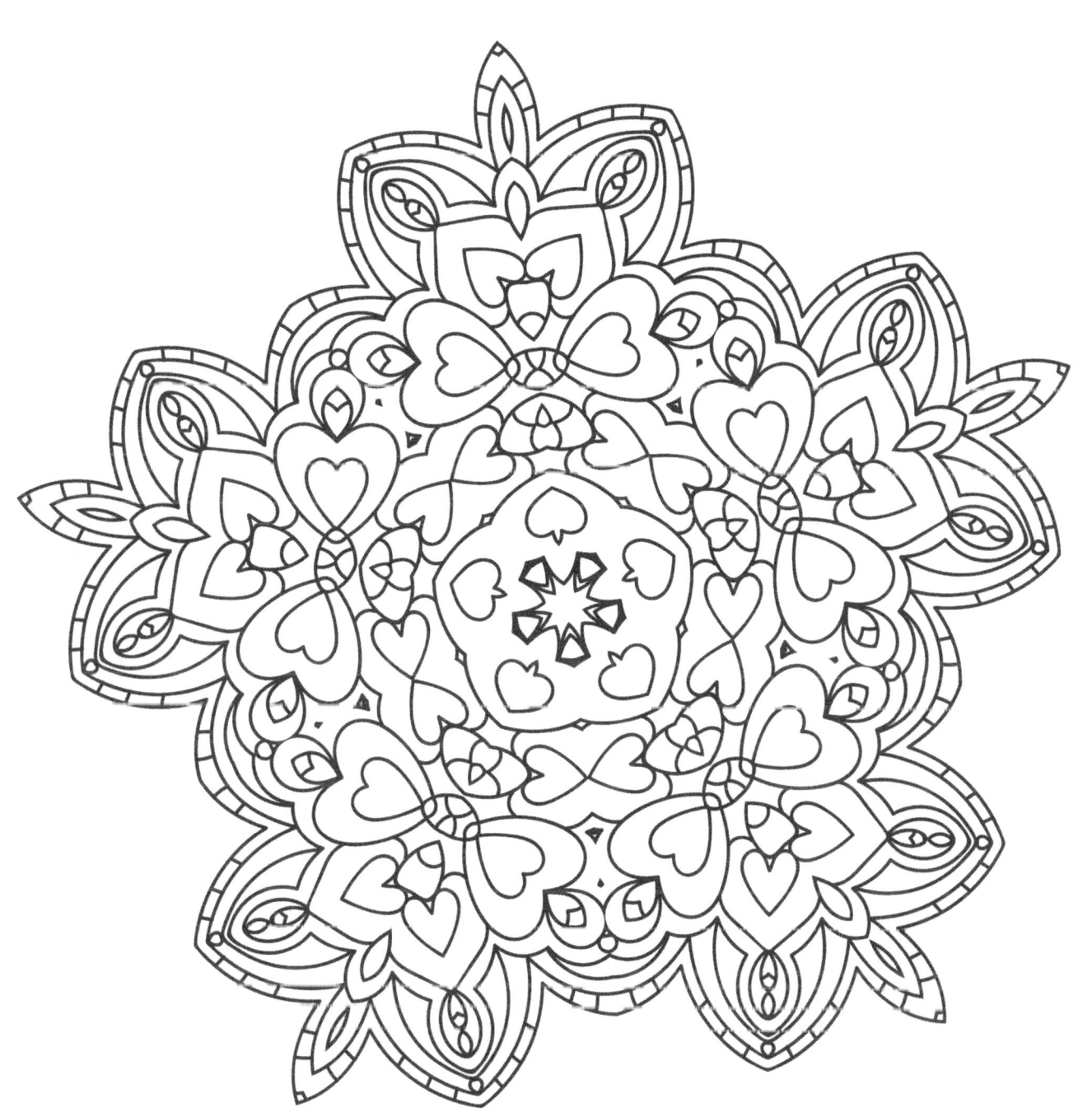

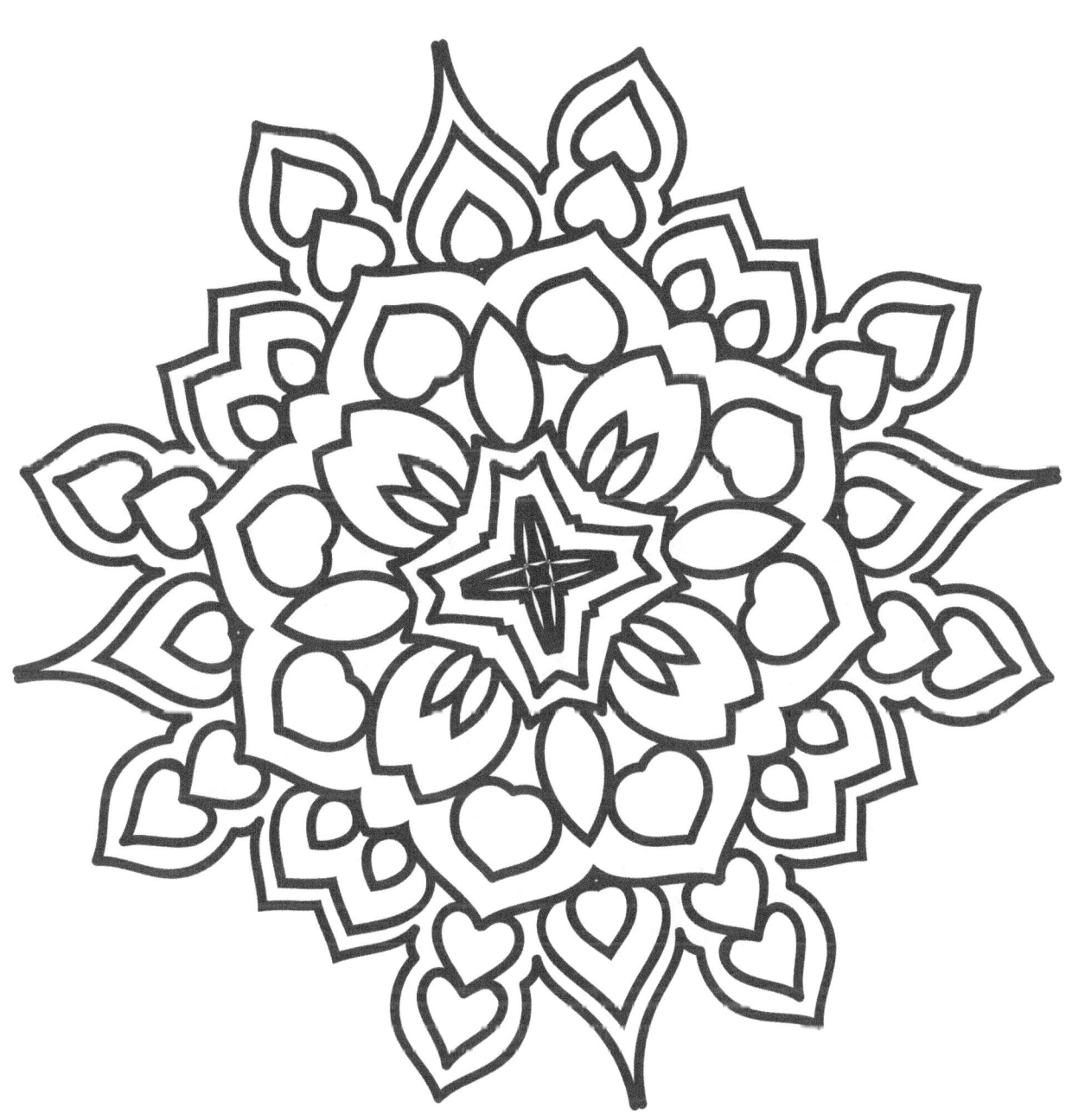

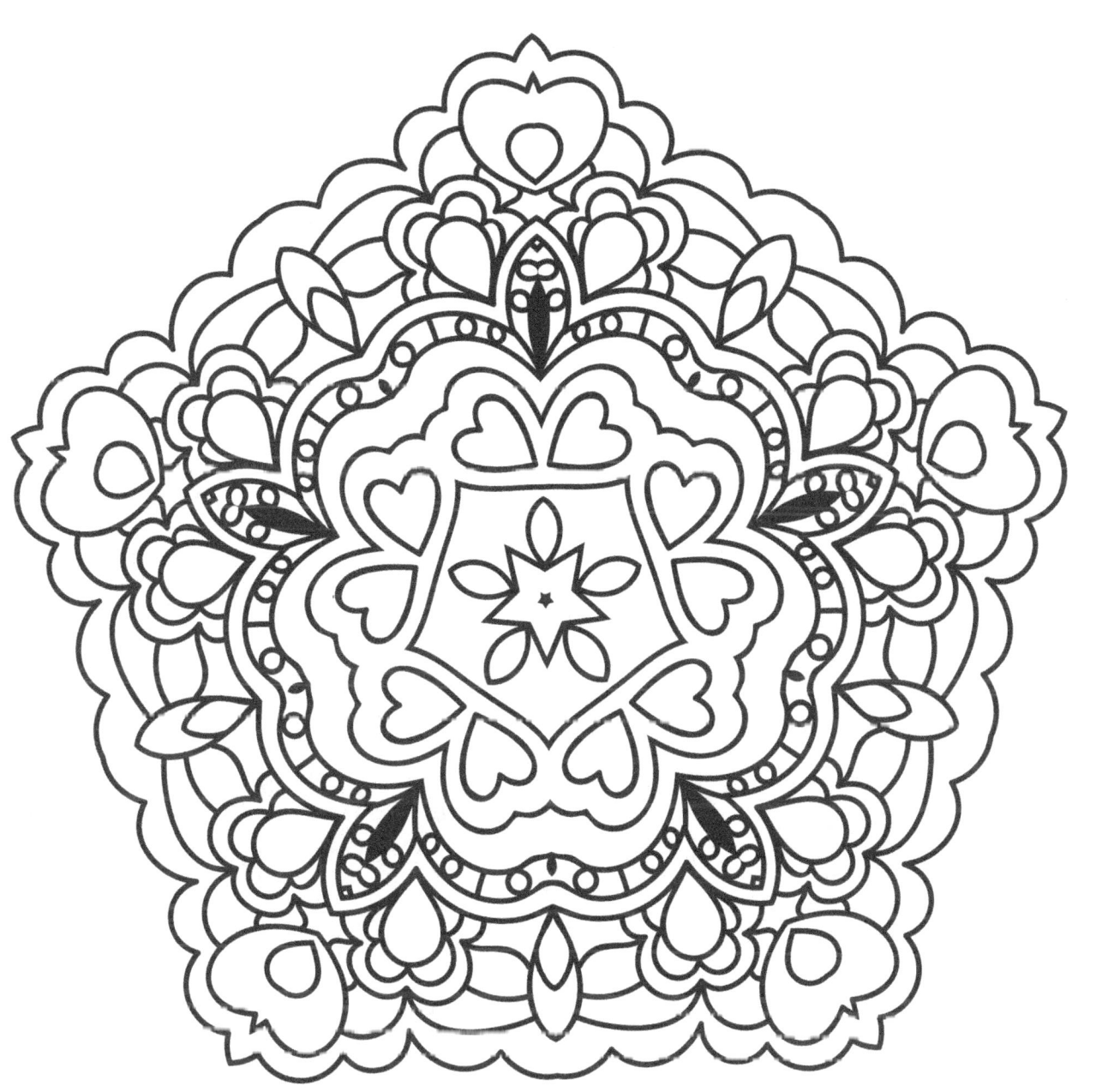

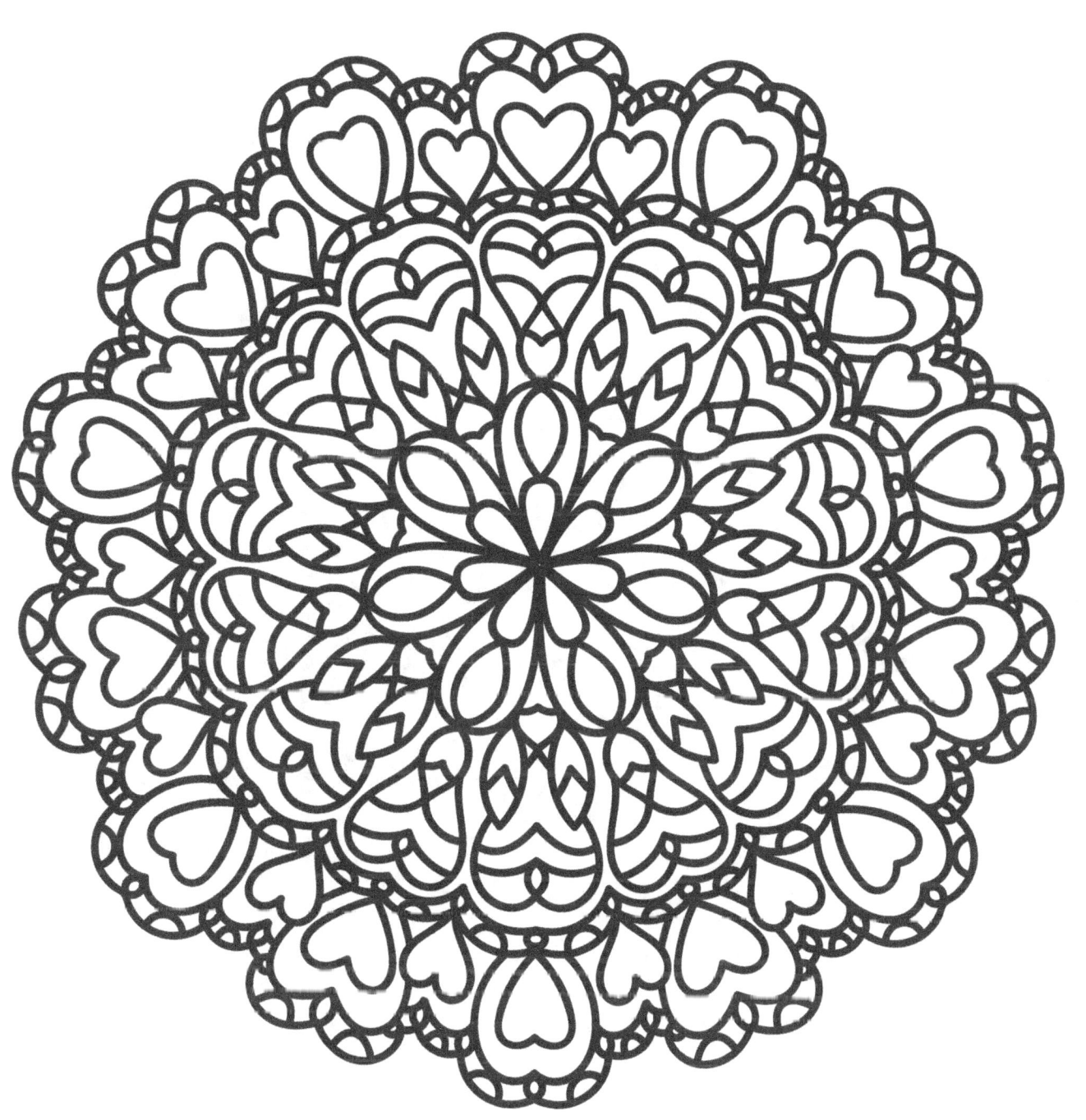

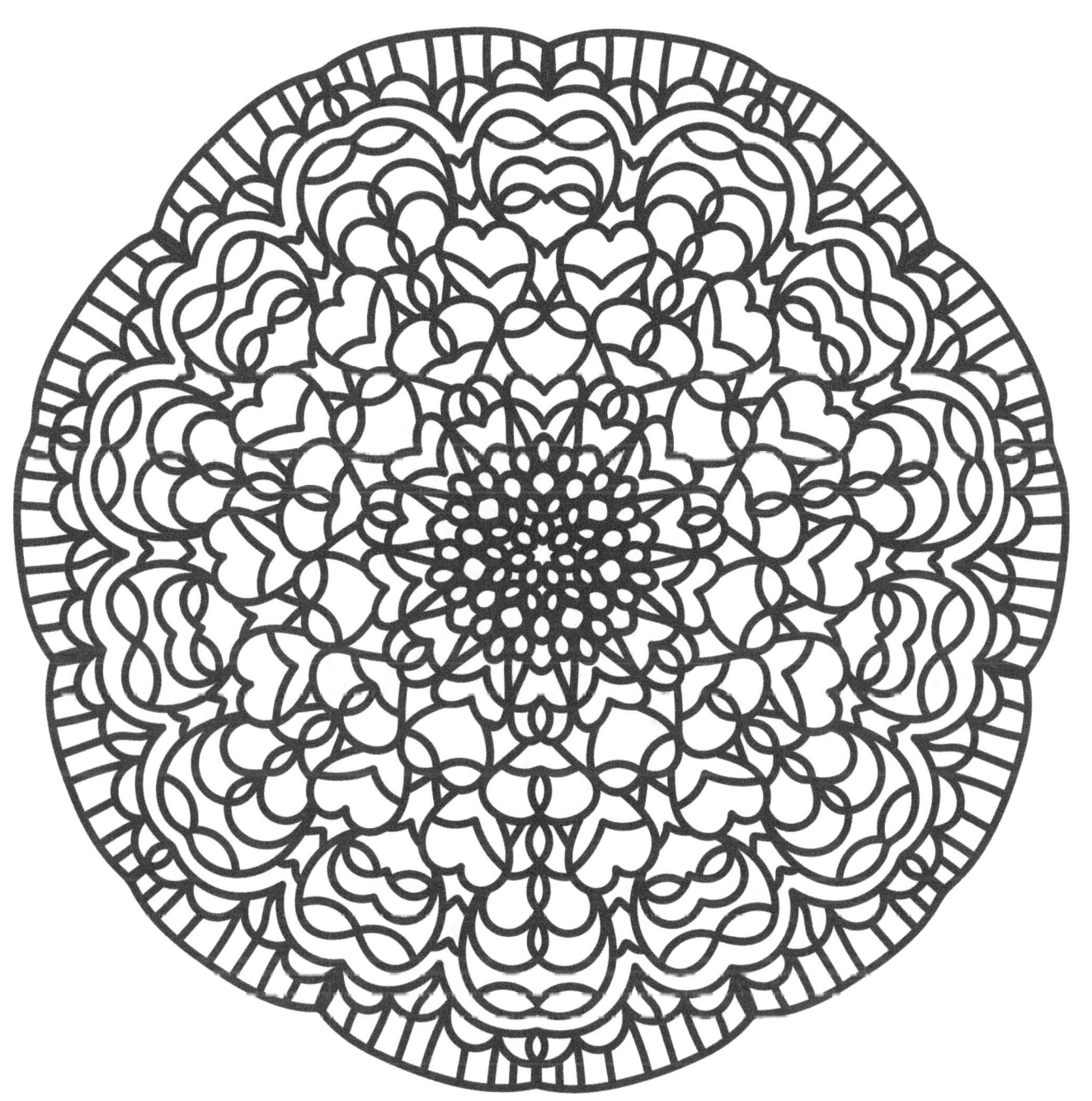

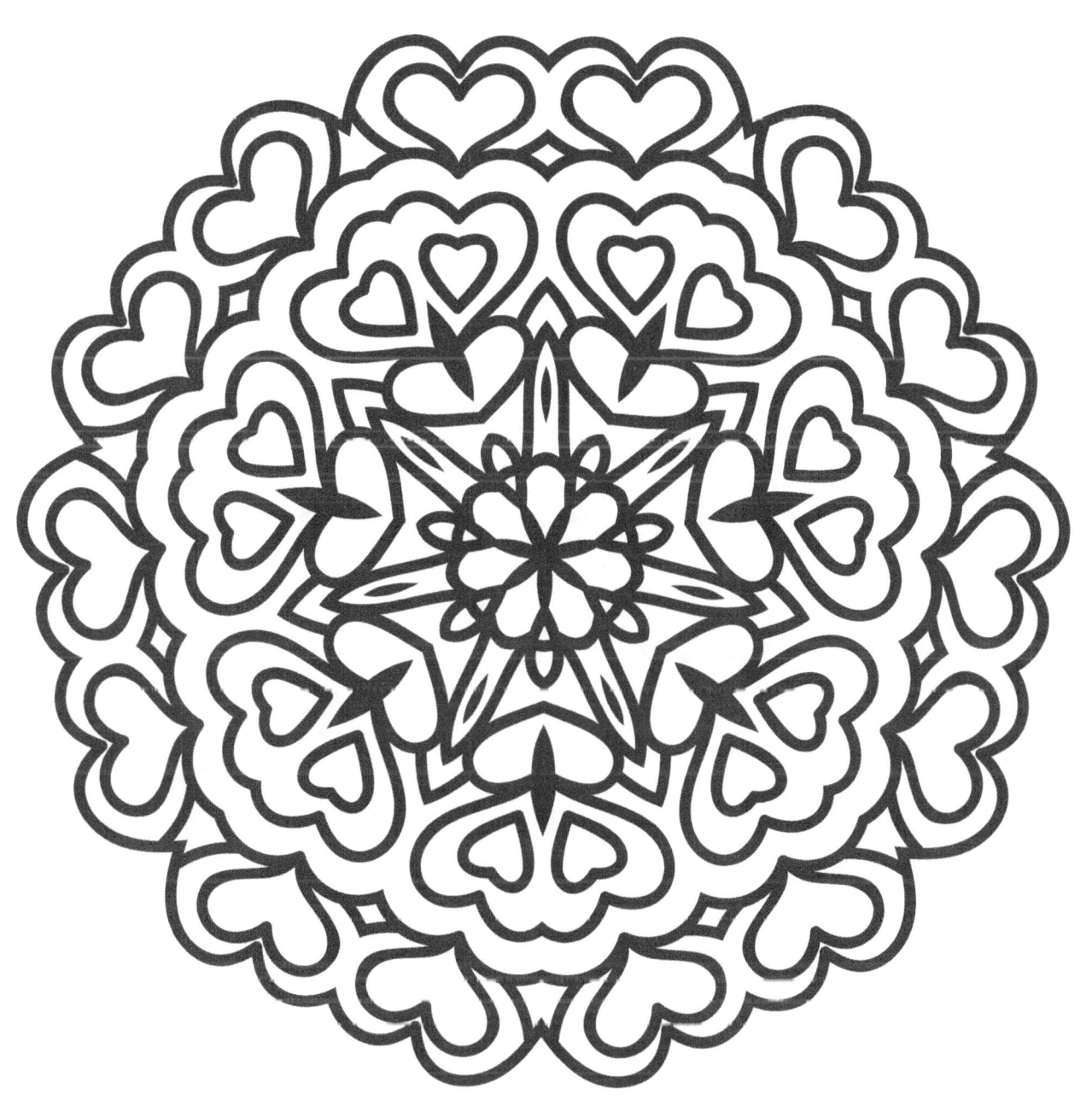

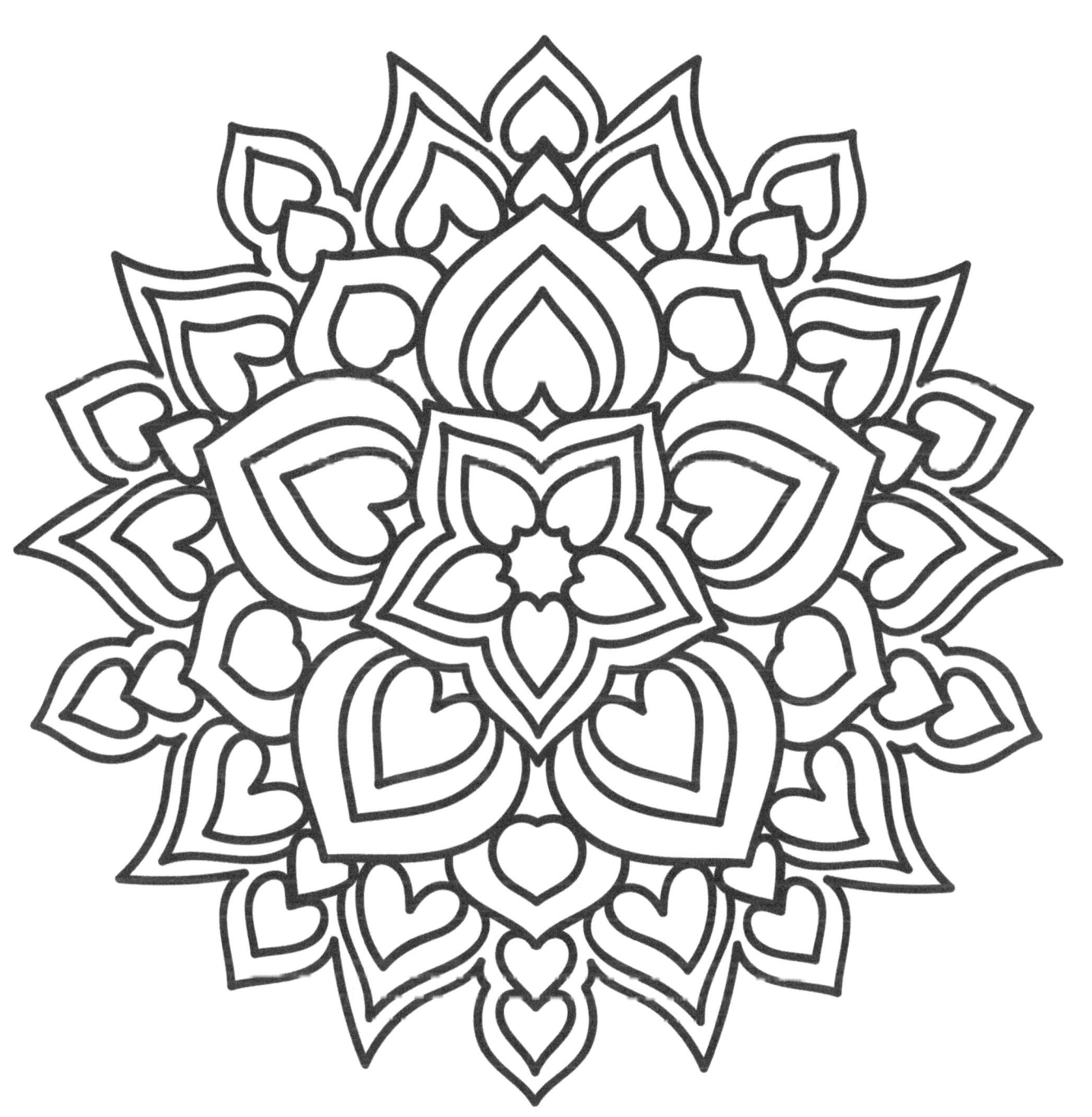

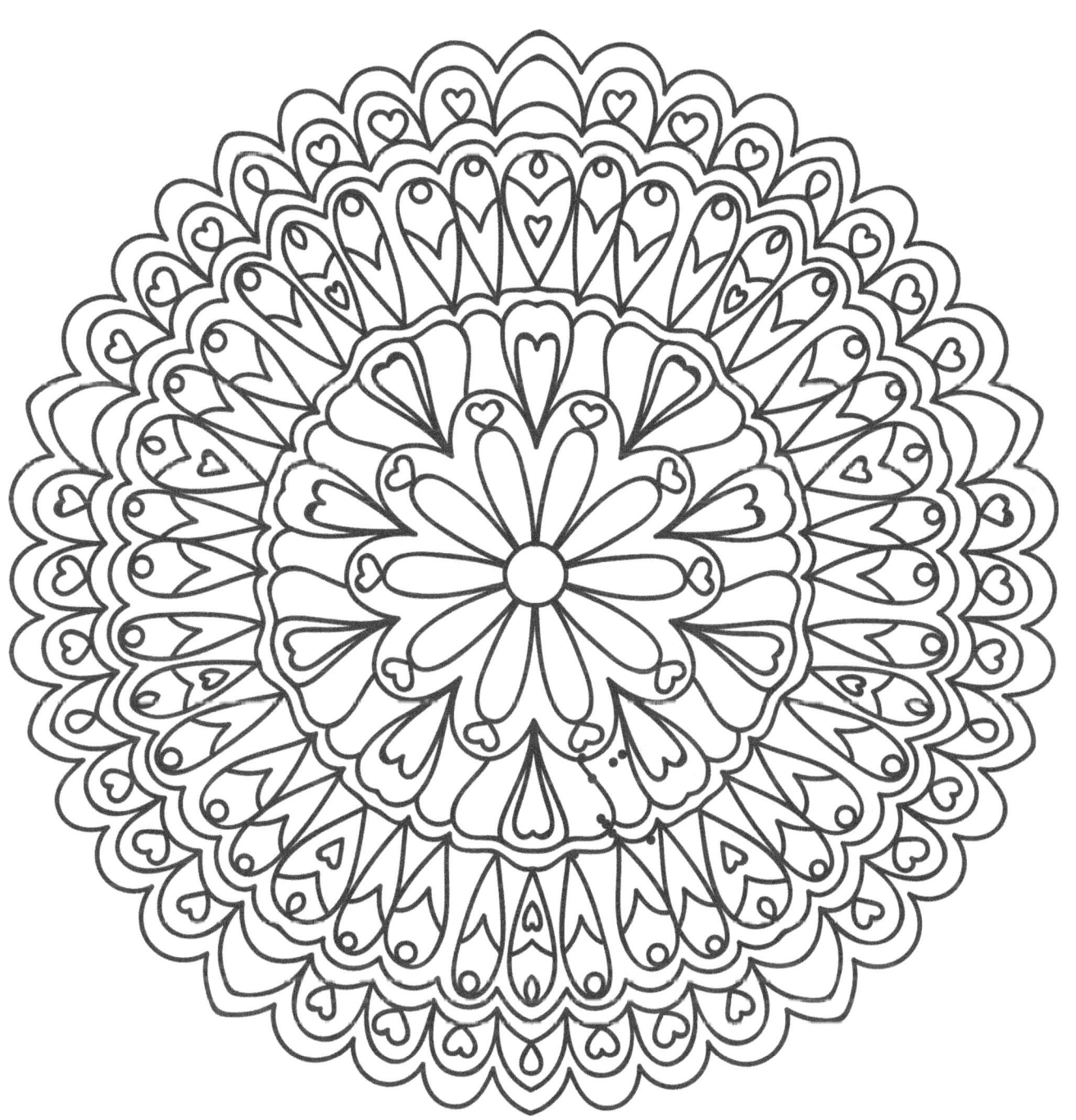

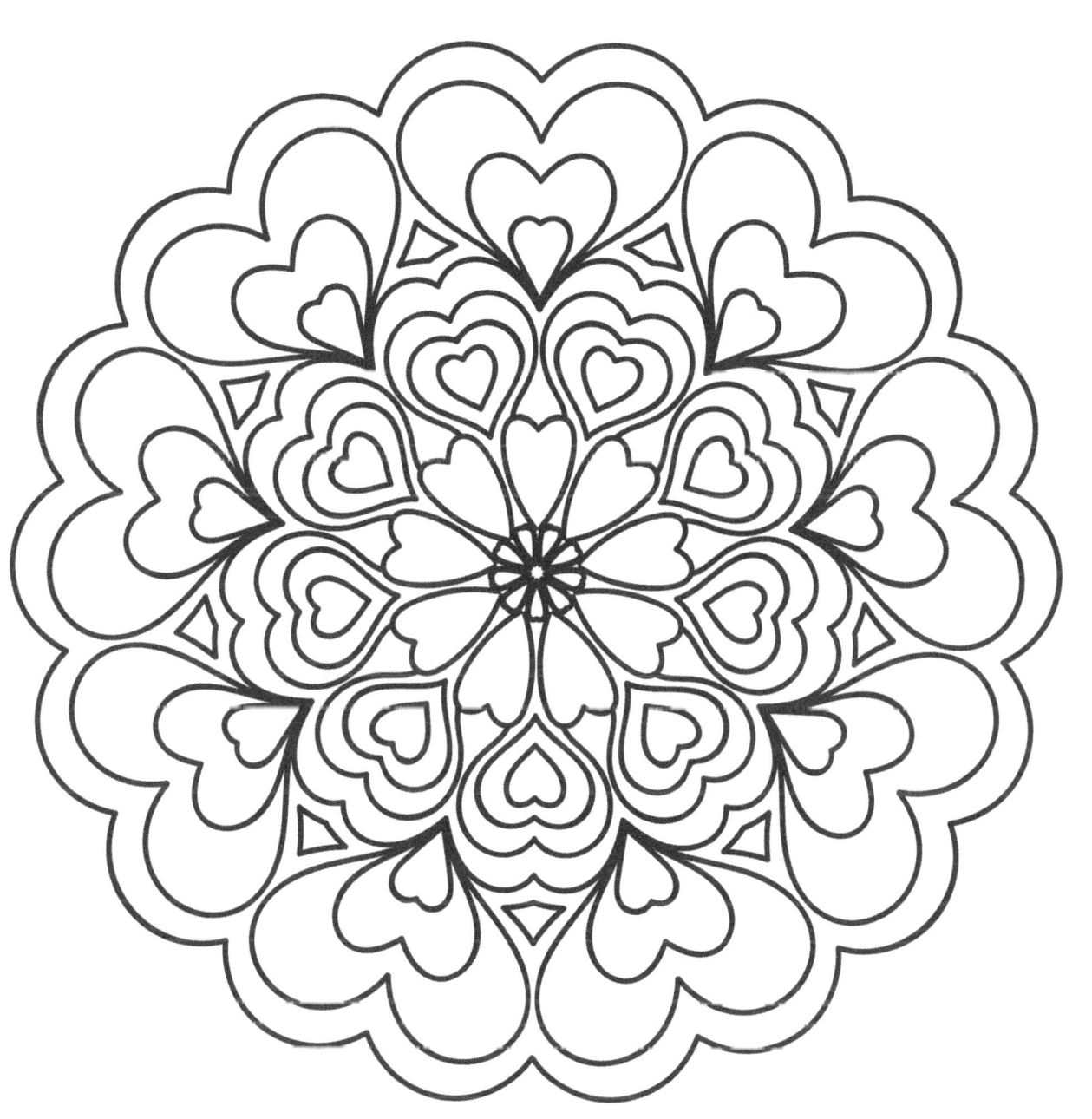

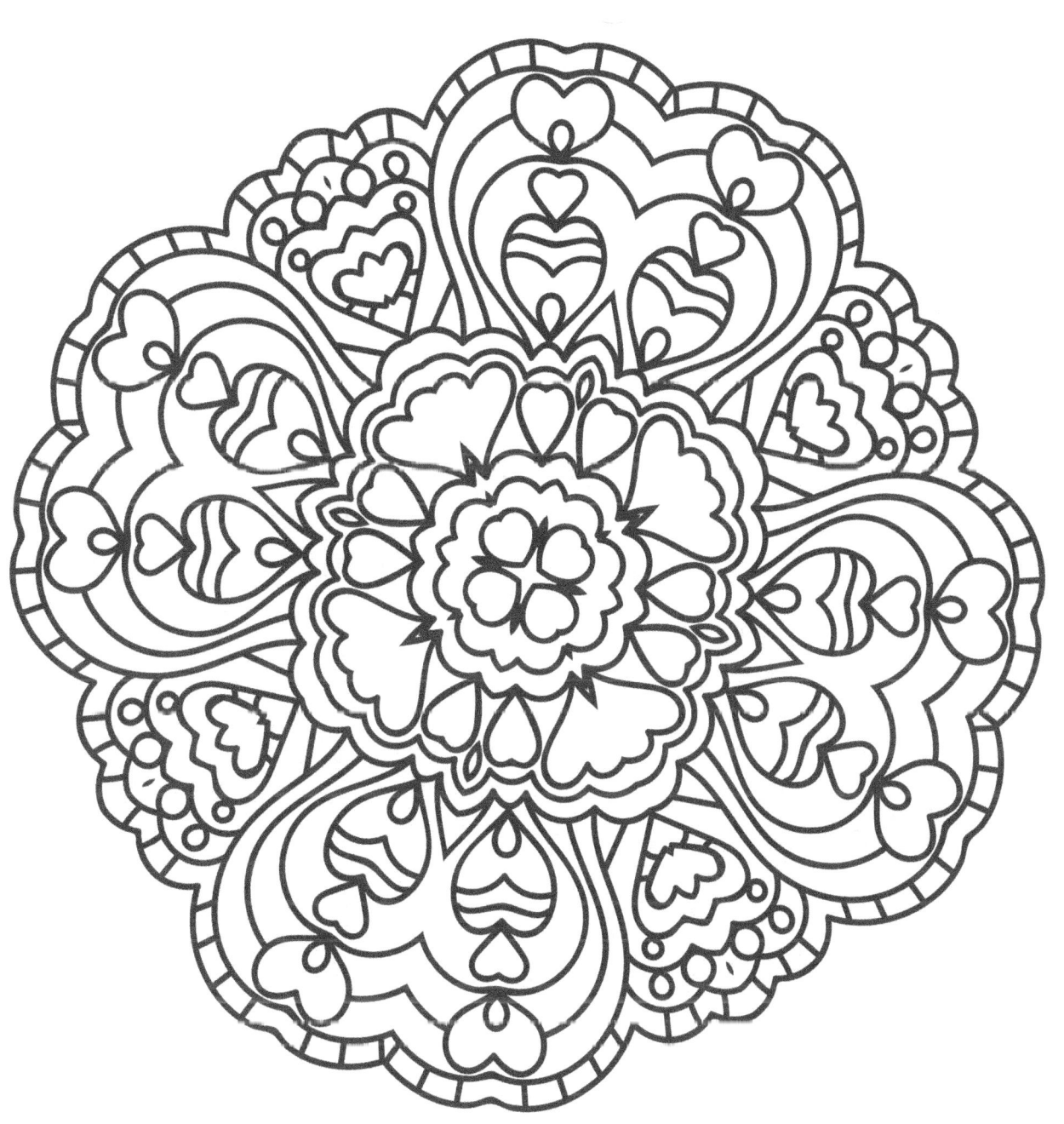

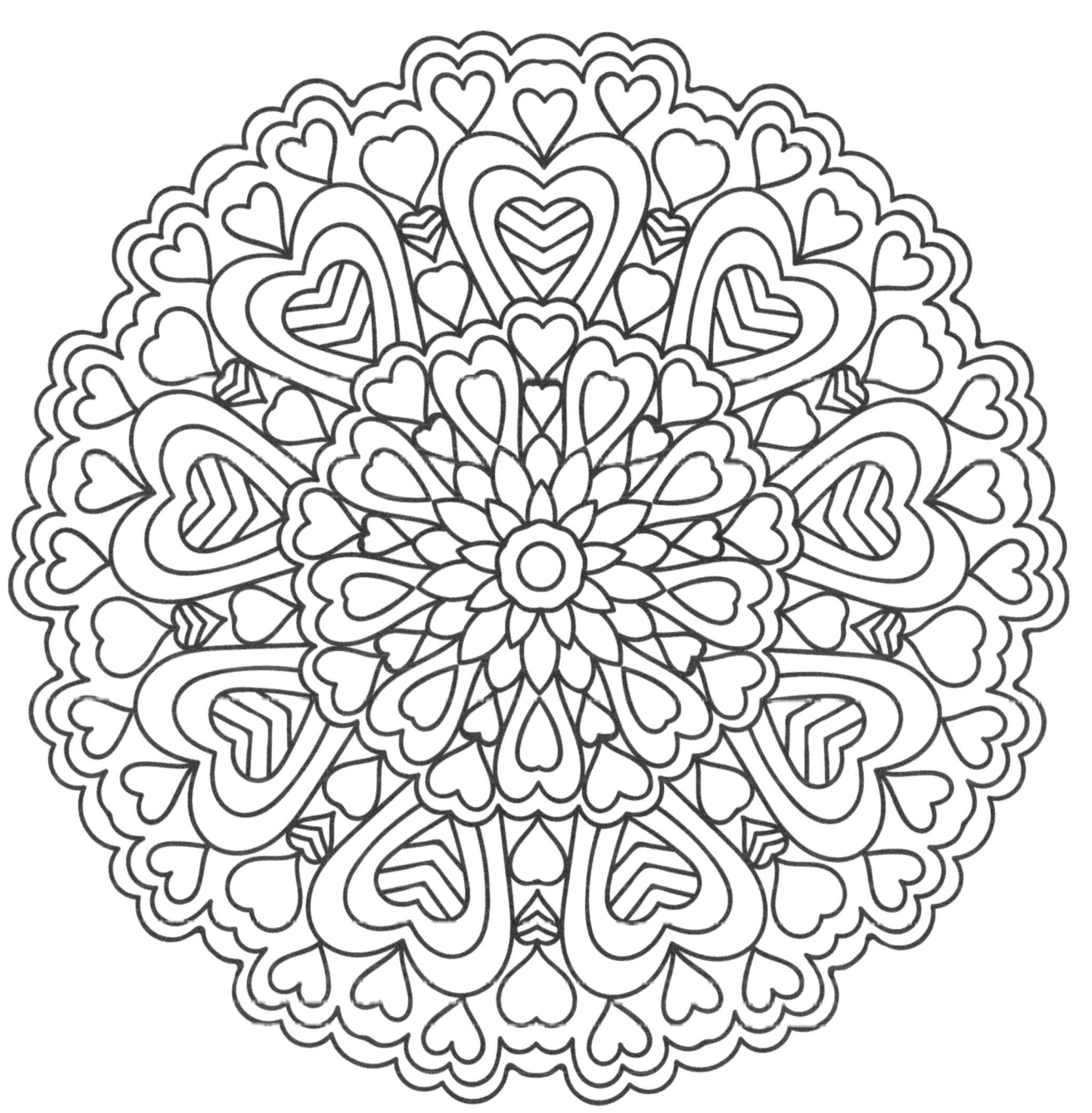

COLOR TEST PAGE

COLOR TEST PAGE

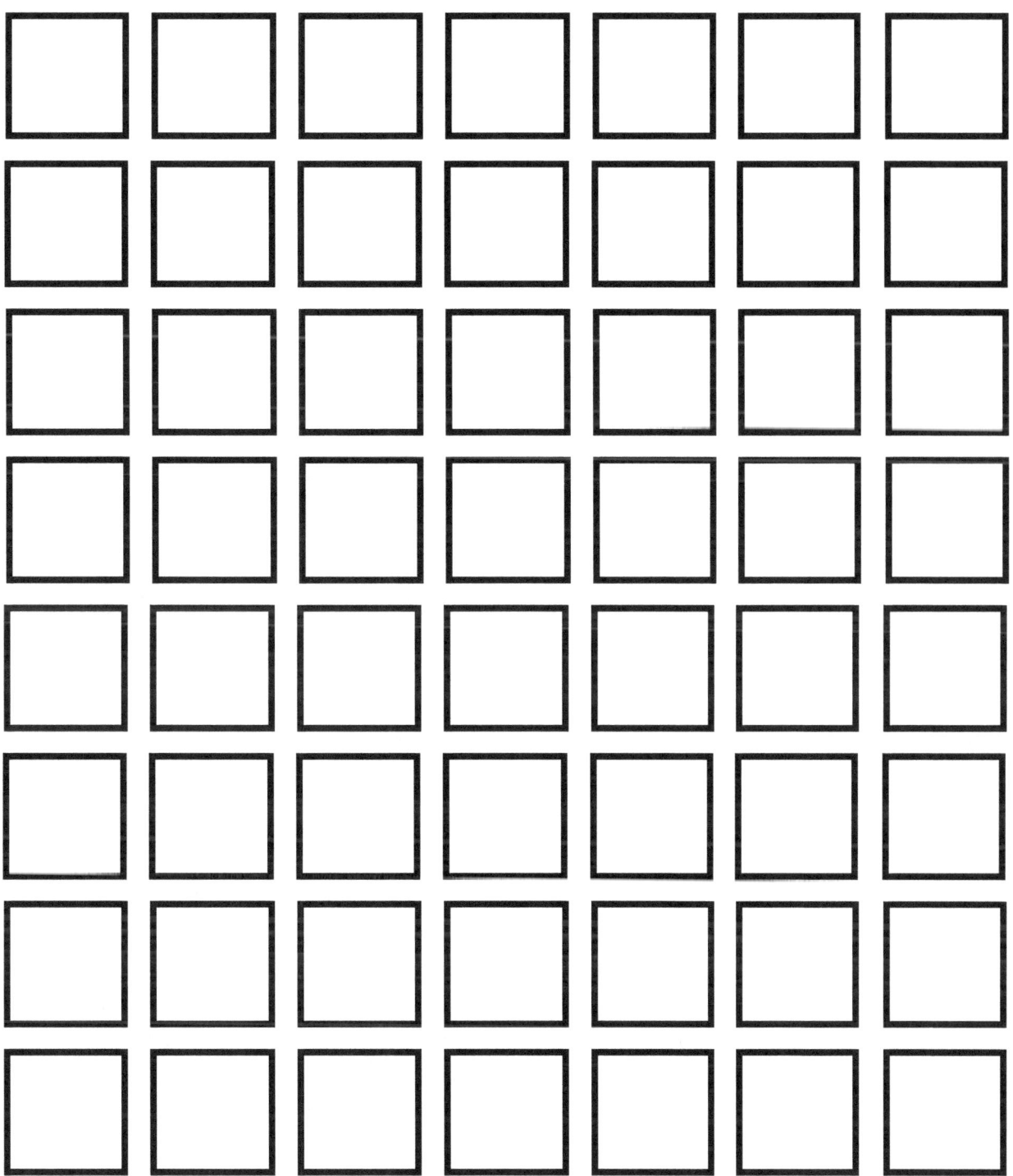

www.ingramcontent.com/pod-product-compliance
Lightning Source LLC
Chambersburg PA
CBHW081615220526
45468CB00010B/2893